Midnight Express

Howard Mahmood

THE FOLLOWING IS BASED ON A TRUE STORY.
IT OCTOBER 6, 1970 ISTANBUL, TURKEY SOUND UNDER, SHARP:
CRACKLE - RIP - SNIP...
FADE IN:

A SET OF CLOTHES ON A HOTEL ROOM BED -- trenchcoat, bulky white turtle-neck sweater, T-shirt, jeans, Western style boots. SOUNDS continue, Accentuated. MOVE Across open TRAVEL BAGS On The bed. Clothes, possessions. CONTINUE Across FURNITURE, WASHBASIN, TOILET...A large room, high old ceilings And windows suggesting Ancient Europe & design, A haunting greenish AFTERNOON light. We MOVE to HANDS, TIGHT - drawing out a strip of adhesive tape, SCISSORS move in TIGHT...SNIP!

UNDERARM, TIGHT. Tape being laid over it.

BACK OF SHOULDER. TIGHT. Tape going on.

BELLYBUTTON, TIGHT. TAPE going Then: a harsh RIP! SOUND and the tape comes off the bellybutton.

HANDS with new strip of tape. Moving to:

HASHISH PLAQUE. Four of them, thinly pressed. One on top of the other. The HAND wrapping a portion of the TAPE around them and:

BELLY, TIGHT. SOUNDS of BREATHING stop. The belly is sucked in. The TAPE is pulled HARD across, then CLINCHED. We hear F.X. of HEART BEAT--

MOVE UP THE CHEST TO:

BILLY HAYES - 21, baby-face, attractive, medium build an aura of innocence. His eyes moving off his belly to: MIRROR. FULL SHOT. Climax. A creature in a bondage of his own devise, he is naked in his underpants, his body criss-crossed by a network of TAPE and 40 tightly pressed plaques of HASHISH in every conceivable crevice of his body. The eyes are hard.

NIX THROUGH HEART BEAT, SOUNDS OF AIRPORT. CUT:
INTERIOR

ISTANBUL AIR TERMINAL dirty, crowded, wooden benches, peddlers. Turkish flight instructions on LOUDSPEAKER, followed by mediocre English translations. NOTE: ALL

DIALOGUE IN TURKISH TO FOLLOW WILL BE MARKED OFF BY PARENTHESIS. A CERTAIN WILL BE SUBTITLED, BUT SOME NOT. LOUDSPEAKER VOICE

Pan American Flight 1 to Frankfurt, London, and New York has arrived and will be ready for boarding at Gate 7 in 20 minutes.

REPEAT IN ENGLISH over: BILL walking down a long CORRIDOR. He moves somewhat stuffly in the clothes we saw laid out on the bed; his face complicated by dark, rather ridiculous aviator sunglasses and an increasing edge of nervousness to his actions. With him is: SUSAN 23, healthy outdoor looks, dressed casually colorful like an American student abroad.

2

APPROACHING P.O.V. a group of TURKISH SECURITY GUARDS, in rumpled green uniforms, at a security CHECKPOINT inspect the carry-on bags of several PASSENGERS.

BILLY tensely contemplating the guards as he walks.

SUSAN digging in her bag for her passport as she walks.

BILLY, looking from guards ahead to SUSAN. He suddenly breaks stride, still a fair distance from the checkpoint. SUSAN glances at him. He is holding his belly.

BILLY
I think I've been poisoned.

SUSAN
And you ate two baclavas, right? I not to touch them, mine was awful.

BILLY
(his voice strained)
Look, I think I'm going to have to go to the john again. You go on through, I'll catch up.
With a sense of panic, he turns and goes back down the corridor without waiting for a response. SUSAN concerned, moves on.

CUT:
BILLY in the WASHROOM MIRROR, again checks himself out.
His glasses are off, and he has just watered himself down.
But the SOUND of his HEARTBEAT is up, and his nerves are visible in his eyeballs and he knows it. He dabs at the sweat on his sideburns. He closes his eyes, takes a DEEP BREATH. A pause. He puts his dark sunglasses back on.
Turns away from the mirror. No going back now.
ADVANCING P.O.V. - SECURITY CHECKPOINT. The GUARDS again.
Closer, closer, Guns in their HOLSTERS. SOUND of billy's heartbeat,
CLOSE - GUARD smoking a cigarette, bored, uniform, looks at BILLY.

CUT:
The GUARDS again.SOUND of Billy's in a tattered olive

GUARD
Passport!
BILLY PASSPORT. The Guard's tobacco-stained FINGERS take it open it. Basic information on Billy: Birth Date April
17, 1949. Birth Place: Babylon, Long Island. No wife, no minors. Signature.
GUARD gives it back to BILLY.

GUARD
Bag!
BILLY opens his shoulder bag, proffers it. The GUARD tosses it, pushing aside books, grabbing a white plastic dish.

GUARD
Nebu?

BILLY
(Understand the
Turkish expression,
"What's this?")
It's a frisbee.

GUARD
Nebu?

BILLY
A Frisbee.
(makes a throwing gesture of the wrist)
You throw, catch it. Game!
Curious, one of the other GUARDS ambles over looking at the frisbee.
BILLY tightens. Cursing the frisbee. Sweat now runs his sideburns again.
HEARTBEAT up.

2ND GUARD
American game. Baseball.

GUARD
Ah!
(puzzled, turns the
Frisbee around and around)
THE SECOND GUARD studies BILLY curious about the sweat.
Suddenly reaches up, indicates the eyes.

GUARD
Take off the glasses.
BILLY understanding the gesture rather than the words, removes his glasses. His eyes.
Straight, staring at the
GUARD without trying to look away. A long moment.
FIRST GUARD stuffs the frisbee back into the bag. Scowls.
Takes a puff on his cigarette, coughs. Phlegm rattles around in his throat.
Reads the International Herald Tribune, seated on a crowded olive-colored out on the
tarmac She has saved him a seat and pulls her bag off as BILLY sits down.

FIRST GUARD
Aaaah!
He waves BILLY through.
BILLY puts his glasses walks past the back the SECOND GUARD turns away. BILLY
walks past the Checkpoint. His HEARTBEAT drops.

4

SUSAN reads the International Herald Tribune, seated on an crowded olive-colored BUS out on the tarmac. She has save him a seat and pulls her bag off as BILLY sits down.

SUSAN
Are you all right?
He looks at her. Relief. A smile, awkward - he wishes he could tell her.

BILLY
Yeah... Yeah.
Lays his head back on the wooden bench. Reaches out:
TAKES HER HAND in his. She returns the grip.
THE BUS DOOR slams shut.
THE TURKISH BUS DRIVER rolls the bus out towards the PLANES visible in the far distance?.
SUSAN, feeling Billy is better, shows him the Herald
Tribune.

SUSAN
(saddened)
D'you see this? Janis Joplin died yesterday.
BILLY, his sunglasses removed, looks at the paper, almost abstractedly.

SUSAN (OFF)
Overdose, in a Hollywood motel.
NEWSPAPER Picture of JANIS JOPLIN. That big, earthy, rugged smile.
BILLY'S P.O.V. - Moves Up page One To The Headline: NIXON

OUT-RAGED AT PALESTINIAN HIJACKERS: CALLS FOR CAPITAL PUNISHMENT
SUSAN
(a faint voice)
Never Was anybody like Janis.
BILLY, thinking other happier things, reaches over and playful!.:squeezes her tit twice, rapidly.

BILLY
(smiles)
Never was anybody like you...

SUSAN
(annoyed, brushes his hand away ,a clicking sound in her throat)
You can't take anything seriously.

BILLY
(smiles)

You're right.

Bus stops suddenly. BILLY changes expression.

THROUGH FRONT WINDSHIELD we see TURKISH SOLDIERS in several HALFTRACKS drawn up in a semicircle blocking the bus. The Pan American PLANE is directly behind. Also JEEPS and a POLICEMAN waving the bus down.

BUS BOOR opens and the Turkish Police OFFICER hops aboard briskly:

OFFICER
Attention please, Ladies and
Gentlemen. For your own safety we're conducting a security check before you board your airplane,
Kindly file out the back. Women and children in one line. Men in another.
PASSENGERS. A confused hum.

VARIOUS PASSENGERS
What's he saying? I don't know...
Marian. Hey Marian, what the hell...
The Turkish-speaking PASSENGERS are gathering together their items and beginning to exit as:
POLICE OFFICER repeats, in ENGLISH

POLICE OFFICER
Idem.
CLOSE BILLY. The POLICE OFFICER is only beginning the speech.in English but already Billy realizes, And it's panic. Silent panic. That horrendous cold feeling all over his back: Oh God what have I done, what can I do now?
He freezes.
MOVE TO SUSAN rising, fetching her things, irritated.

SUSAN
Jesus, they do everything ass backwards in Turkey.
Behind her we see the other AMERICAN PASSENGERS beginning to disembark with the usual chorus of overlapped conversations, expletives, including:

PASSENGERS
They're checking for hijackers.
Any Palestinians aboard? Hey Harry, get rid of your grenades...
Laughter is returned from several of the American contingent, but we MOVE BACK to BILLY in foreground; all of a sudden he is on his knees trying to crawl under the seat.

SUSAN (OFF)
Billy, what's the matter?

BILLY
My passport!

SUSAN
No!
She bends down to look, coming FACE TO FACE with him. He grips her arm.

BILLY
(low voice)
Susan - forget it. Go get us a seat on the plane. Now.

SUSAN
(picking up the real fear in his voice)
What is it? . . . Billy?

BILLY
(a fierce whisper, panic)
For Christ's sake, just GET on the plane, okay!
His tone stuns her; never before has he spoken to her like that. A LOOK between them; he has his glasses off now.
She's not a stupid girl by any means and realizes something is very wrong and for the both of them, she'd best do exactly as he says. And fast. She moves OUT OF SHOT.
BILLY, crouched low in the aisle starts to work fast, his finger: shaking reaching into his sweater starting to work the TAPE loose from around his chest; looking from under the bench. Still quite a bit of commotion as passengers are exiting. BUT THEN:
BILLY P.O.V. - UNIFORMED LEGS coming slowly down Isle
Towards him. The muzzle of An M-l RIFLE tapping loosely
Against the side of the kneecap.
PAN WITH and MOVE UP as TURKISH MILITARY LIEUTENANT comes into view, intersecting outgoing PASSENGERS, eyes casually coming to rest on:
BILLY looks up from his kneeling position on floor; his sweater rolled back down; he indicates the passport in his hand. "Just found it" expression.
MOVE to the LIEUTENANT not necessarily suspecting anything, but with a customary insolence reserved for young vagrant- types, he stretches his rifle arms length with one hand and gently prods Billy up with the tip of the muzzle placed under his chin. MOVE BACK to the OFFICER, bringing the rifle back to his side, indicating Billy get off the bus with the others. All in silence.

CUT:
BILLY among a group of MALE PASSENGERS funnelling into two lines that pass on either side of a wooden inspection table.
Thirty TURKISH SOLDIERS with rifles ring the area. It is open, vast, no place to run or hide. The only apparent hope is to melt into their regular jostling patterns of the passengers impatiently waiting.
TWO PLAINCLOTHESMEN (Police) are on each side of the table, body-searching the male passengers alternately.
SUSAN is in a similar set-up twenty yards away, with FEMALE

ATTENDANTS doing the searching. She glances at Billy as she undergoes search. She is cleared, passes on, towards the ramp of the plane.

BILLY, his sunglasses off, smoothly melts among the male

PASSENGERS pulling some books from his shoulder bag. Glides to the head of the line. MOVE TO:

The FIRST OFFICER patting down a PASSENGER, his back partially turned to Billy. MOVE AROUND bringing him into foreground as:

BILLY skirts him in the background, camouflaged among two other conversing PASSENGERS waiting for the SECOND OFFICER who now appears in foreground on the lateral TRACK; he is busy with another passenger. In passing him, Billy replaces the books in his shoulder bag as though he had already been searched by the first officer, Tension. FOLLOW BILLY as he approaches the boarding ramp.

BILLY P.O.V. - SUSAN at the top of the ramp waiting.

Smiling STEWARDESSES. Pan America. Haven.

BILLY - FOOT rising off Turkish soil onto ramp.

TURKISH HAND lightly touching Billy's elbow, then grasping the ARM.

TURK (OFF)
Just a minute!
BILLY his eyes flattening.
SUSAN in LONG SHOT, reacting.
BILLY turns trying to seem casual; he confronts the SECOND
OFFICER face to face and gestures towards the:
FIRST OFFICER who happens to glance at them.

SECOND
Nebu? Did you search him?

FIRST OFFICER
(frowns)
No!
SECOND OFFICER tightens his grip on BILLY, angry, and pulls him back to the TABLE. MOVE with them. The officer has been lied to; in addition he is young, inexperienced, about eighteen.

SECOND OFFICER
(grunts a command, makes a gesture)
BILLY, comprehending, spreads his arms. The OFFICER pats him down carefully, brushing against his armpits. Precisely in the area where we saw the hashish. But incredibly he doesn't notice, continuing to work his way down the hips and legs.
CLOSE BILLY eyes on the sky behind the OFFICER, praying silently for a break.
TURKISH FINGERS moving up the inside of his legs, onto his belly, touching the hard bulge below the navel. But again not noticing.
BILLY in limbo, SOUND of his heartbeat.
SECOND OFFICER pausing, his fingers around Billy's chest, about to let it go, then:
PLACES HIS HAND suddenly flat on Billy's heart.

OFFICER, sensing the accelerated Heartbeat, stares at:
BILLY whose eyes jump, startled by this technique.
FINGERS like excited spiders quickly run back up into the armpit area. STOP - right on the packets.
TURKISH EYES SWIVEL to BILLY EYES CLOSE. Frozen moment.
Then, sudden blur of movement at the edge of frame.
SECOND OFFICER jumping back, grabbing his pistol from his holster, crouching on one knee, aiming the gun barrel at
BILLY, hand shaking. He is terrified.

SECOND OFFICER
(screaming)
Bomb! He's got a bomb!
AMERICAN PASSENGERS scream and the deck all around.

AMERICAN PASSENGER
Bomb! Bomb!
BILLY stands there, arms straight up in the air, eyes clamped shut, trying not to breathe.
CHORUS of rifle and revolver CLICKS OFF as:
PULL BACK to OVERHEAD SHOT BILLY surrounded by thirty
SOLDIERS with rifles pointed at him from all directions, crouched nervously. The PASSENGERS all huddled on the ground.
BILLY, eyes closed. Edge of frame shows a shaky muzzle a
REVOLVER poked into his belly, moving up.
MOVE to THE FIRST OFFICER, older, more experienced but scared, poking with the revolver; reaches in with his hand cautiously, starts to pull up the turtleneck sweater.
MOVE with the hand, revealing the HASHISH PLAQUES around the navel. A pause.
His HAND draws the sweater higher. More

PLAQUES.
FIRST OFFICER'S FACE relaxes. Starts to smile, finding it funny.

FIRST OFFICER
(yells out)
It's hashish. just a smuggler.

SOLDIERS (OFF)
(in chorus echo, relaxing, chuckling)
Hashish...smuggler...hippy...
MASTER ANGLE SOLDIERS REGROUPING. PASSENGERS starting to rise from the ground.
SUSAN dumbfounded watching all this from the door of the
PLANE, starts back down the ramp. But a flow of upcoming
PASSENGERS slows her descent.

BILLY is led roughly by TWO SOLDIERS parallel to the plane his hands on his head. He manages a glance at Susan. A slight but strong movement of the head and eyes. 'No. Don't come down the stairs'
SUSAN understands it, looks helplessly, hesitates lost between two worlds. A silent shaping of a puzzled mouth.

SUSAN
...Billy...?
She is washed back along in the flow of passengers.

CUT:
VIP ROOM AIRPORT LOUNGE. The scene moves very fast,
Indicating A sense of chaos. Much smoke. Many phone calls.
Half A dozen Turkish police OFFICERS Are bizarrely seated
In A row of fold up chairs next to A desk. Chattering among themselves (AD LIB) lighting their Turkish cigarettes.
They hardly pay attention as:
MOVE TO BILLY, scared, sweating - backlit by the huge windows overlooking the airstrip. In background, we see the 707 Pan American PLANE beginning to circle towards the runway. GUARDS have stripped him down to his bare chest and now knife through the adhesive tape from two sides at once. Then RIP the tape off. BILLY winces.
ANOTHER ANGLE the room. Billy's luggage Is being Tossed.
Clothes fly through the air. A sweatshirt; Marquette
University Rowing Team. A 35mm camera. A gift package for his mother ripped open. A silver Turkish kettle, clanging
To The floor. Another package is ripped open and a set of
Turkish tea cups smash and break all over the floor. Very fast.
BILLY watches, bewildered. He is stripped of the last plaque in of the confusion is that each time another police officer his navel. FOLLOW the plaque clattering onto the pile of forty plaques.

FIRSTOFFICER (OFF)
Name?

BILLY (OFF)
William Hayes.
MOVE BACK QUICKLY to the OFFICER with notebook at the desk.
Part of the confusion is that each time we see another police officer we see he has another face.

FIRST OFFICER
Vi... Vilyum... Vilyum...

BILLY (OFF)
Hayes.
FIRST OFFICER

Hi-yes...
(writes it down)

ANOTHER ANGLE --
FIRST OFFICER
'Merican?

BILLY
(nods)
New York.
The OFFICER is puzzled.

BILLY
New York... New York...

FIRST OFFICER
Ahhhh...Nev Yok!
(writes it down)

A LOUD SOUND OFF.
The DOOR flies open and ANOTHER OFFICER strides in.
Paunchy, moustached. The room is suddenly silent as we
TRACK him in, followed by a grinning civilian FLUNKY with a big portable photo
instrument and bulb.
THE FIRST OFFICER jumps up from the desk, makes an obsequious salute to the
SECOND OFFICER who arrogantly acknowledges it and takes the vacated chair
behind the desk. The FIRST OFFICER moves to the first fold-up chair in the row,
pushing the police officer in that chair further down. THIS OFFICER, in turn, shoves
the next man down. It goes all the way down the line like a comedy until the last man
in the row stands up against the wall. But this is all in the background as:

SECOND OFFICER
Name?

BILLY
William Hayes.

SECOND OFFICER
Vil... Vilyum...?

BILLY
Hayes...
Sharp SOUND OFF of FILM BEING RIPPED FROM CAMERA. He darts a look at
POLICEMAN stretching the undeveloped film out. Another loud SOUND OFF,
interrupting this--

THE DOOR flies open again and a THIRD OFFICER strides in, obviously the most important yet, because the SECOND OFFICER jumps up from the desk, and all the others immediately move down one seat in the hierarchy without a moment's hesitation. But the THIRD OFFICER strides right up to Billy, waves to the SECOND OFFICER. THE CAMERAMAN in background bubbles with enthusiasm, sliding into position. Billy is puzzled - what's going on? His arm is grabbed and he is swivelled around.

REVERSE ANGLE - OVER CAMERAMAN
BILLY in the middle, flanked by SECOND and THIRD OFFICER, grinning like big game hunters, their arms on his shoulders.
The FIRST OFFICER, sticking a bunch of hashish plaques into Billy's hands, runs OUT OF FRAME. BILLY looks from side to side. The SECOND OFFICER pats him hard on the back of the head, meaning 'look at camera'. BILLY glances at him, sees the grin on both the officers' faces. Thinking this is the necessary expression, he grins at the camera.
CAMERAMAN disgustedly looks up from his eyepiece.

CAMERAMAN
No.. He's smiling. Make him look miserable.
SECOND OFFICER slugs BILLY in the stomach with a quick back-handed fist. BILLY groans, sinks to his knees. The plaques fall on the floor.

FIRST OFFICER
(running up)
Gel? Gel??
He growls, grabbing Billy's arm and hauling him up, gathering the hashish plaques and putting them back in his arms. The TWO OFFICERS put their arms back on Billy's shoulders. BILLY, in pain, makes the proper expression of misery.
FLASH! The bulb goes.

CUT:
THE 707 PAN AMERICAN PLANE, destination New York, roars up into the sky. PULL BACK all the way to BILLY sitting next to the window, huddled over, feeling woozy and near vomiting. He glimpses the plane but it is anti-climatic now; as he stares down at his boots. Then remembers something! Surprised.
ANOTHER ANGLE - ROOM. The Turkish OFFICERS talk AD LIB among themselves, congratulating, slapping shoulders, pointing to the hashish plaques, etc.
In center background, we see BILLY submissively lifting his arm for permission to speak,
THIRD OFFICER nods, approaches, followed by OTHERS.
BILLY slowly, partly out of pain, pulls off one of his boots, bangs it on the heel and two more PLAQUES clatter to the floor.
TURKISH MOUTHS drop open.
BILLY finishes the process with the other boot. An awkward silence OFF.

BILLY

(trying to explain, innocent)
I forgot... I really did.
(makes ineffective gestures)
ANOTHER ANGLE. The room explodes with screams and commotion.

AD LIB:
THIRD OFFICER
(screaming at SECOND

OFFICER)
You idiot, you fool. You told me the American was searched... and he's pulling hashish out of his boots! You're all dogshit!

SECOND OFFICER
(turning on First
Officer, screaming)
You worthless piece of garbage, where did you learn to search a prisoner? He's been in our custody for an hour, etc.

FIRST OFFICER
(screaming at the others)
Who searched him? Who?
Amid all the screaming TWO POLICEMEN rush over and yank
BILLY upwards, and start to strip all his clothes.

BILLY
(protesting)
That's it! That's all I have!

CUT:
BILLY spread-eagled STARK NAKED against the wall. He is afraid to move. A strange silence.
ANOTHER ANGLE. BILLY naked in center B.G. against the wall. The OFFICERS and SOLDIERS quietly leering at his trim, muscular buttocks. Hungry stares. Bisexuality is prevalent in Turkey. But there is also embarrassment among the officers; none would do anything openly in front of the others; instead they just stare and smoke their cigarettes. Low murmurs. Continued telephone calls. Much thick smoke all over the room.
Another DOOR opens OFF. Obsequious GREETINGS in Turkish.
BILLY is afraid to look over his shoulder, feeling enormously humiliated.

VOICE (OFF)
Howdy, Billy. Howya doing, Ok?
A perfect Texas drawl. BILLY glances over his shoulder.
Sees:
TEX a tall, lanky blonde-haired American in a business suit with boots. Clean cut, very handsome, with a strong flavour of danger in his blue eyes.

13

TEX
(smiling, extends
Billy's clothes)
I think these gentlemen have finished for the time being if you'd like to put your clothes
on.
ANOTHER ANGLE - BILLY, so grateful at last to see a fellow
American, reaches quietly for the clothes, his eyes never leaving Tex. Release?

CUT:
TURKISH DETECTIVE sits at the main desk in the room. Unlike the others, he has no
moustache; a skeletal face, intelligent looking. TEX Is behind, leaning casually up
against the wall. Angled to Billy's side is the entire array of seated OFFICERS looking
on like a tribunal.

DETECTIVE
(thickly accented
English, sympathetic)
Are you afraid, Vilyum?
BILLY, standing to the side of the desk, clothed now, buckling his belt - afraid.

BILLY
No, I'm not afraid.

DETECTIVE
Good. There's nothing to be afraid of. If you co-operate with us, you will be on the plane
for New York tomorrow... yes?

BILLY
(softly, hoping)
Yes...?

DETECTIVE
Good. Now, where did you get the hashish?

BILLY
A cabdriver. He picked me up in the Pudding Shoppe in the bazaar.

DETECTIVE
Would you recognize him again?

BILLY
Yes. I think so.

DETECTIVE
Good. Would you go back to the

Pudding Shoppe now and point him out to my men if you see him?

BILLY'S EYES MOVE TO:
TEX who makes a cool affirmative nod of the eyes to Billy.

BILLY (OFF)
Yes.
STREETS, ISTANBUL, AFTERNOON. TEX drives his American CAR;
BILLY in the passenger seat; TWO TURKISH PLAINCLOTHESMEN in the rear seats
. Various BACKGROUND SHOTS of the city.

TEX
(casual tone)
You decided to fly at a bad time
Billy Palestinian Guerrillas all over the place blowing up planes and all.

BILLY
(shakes his head)
Stupid.

TEX
Four planes in four days...but I guess you kids don't read the newspapers...and what
with our people kicking up a shit storm
'bout the flow of heroin from Turkey you got...

BILLY
But didn't have heroin.

TURK
(grins)
Well I'm not up on all that. A drug's a drug seems to me Billy and...

BILLY
(sweating)
But it was my first time. I'm not really a smuggler, was just two kilos.

TEX
Well, you see Billy, it don't really matter right now if it's 2 kilos or 200 kilos. The Turks
love to catch any foreigner smuggling - it shows the world they're fighting the drug
trade.

BILLY
But just...

TEX
Just what?

BILLY

I just needed some extra money. I was broke, the guy offered me the hash and...
It sounds bad. Tex looks at him without expression.
Pause.Billy tries to sense a sympathy in this ambiguous man, a liking towards himself.
But feels nothing yet, except someone who can speak English.

BILLY

...are you with the Consulate?

TEX

(not looking at him)
Something like that. Cigarette?
ANOTHER ANGLE - BILLY nervously takes the pack and matches.

TEX

How much you pay this joker... this cab driver?

BILLY

Two hundred dollars. It was my last two hundred.

TEX

How much did you figure to make?
BILLY fumbles to light up his cigarette. He is nervous, grateful to volunteer any information...anything.

BILLY

Three, four thousand...I don't know. The guy offered me the hash--
(shakes his head)
...it just seemed like easy money.

TEX

Beats working.

BILLY

I was just going to sell it to friends. I'm not a pusher, honest.
TEX grins, sceptical of his naivete, changing the subject.

TEX

Got a family back there?

BILLY

(inhales deeply)
Yeah. Parents, brother, sister.
Babylon, Long Island.

TEX
What's your father do?

BILLY
He sells insurance for Metropolitan
Life.

TEX
(a pause, not looking at Billy)
Be tough on 'em.
BILLY nods, takes a deep drag on his cigarette.

ANOTHER ANGLE
TEX
Girlfriend?

BILLY
...She was on the plane.
Tex glances at him, questioningly.

BILLY
She didn't know anything about...I wouldn't have wanted her to.

TEX
Lucky girl.
Billy leans back in seat, blowing out the cigarette smoke.

BILLY
Jeez, she used to say I was the lucky one.

TEX
Let's hope so, Billy. Let's sure hope so.
A narrow cobblestone STREET. TEX pulls the car to a halt.

CUT:
THE PUDDING SHOPPE TWILIGHT Internationally-known cafe, adjacent
BAZAAR. Crowded, noisy. WOMEN dressed in black hold crying CHILDREN by the
hands. FOREIGNERS, mostly students and hippies, move about laughing, joking.
Hawkers, street peddlers, vendors cooking shishkebab. small GYPSY
BOY leads a huge MUZZLED BEAR on a leash.
BILLY sits at a small outdoor TABLE alone sipping tea and eating baclava - nervous,
very nervous, still trying to sort it all out in his head. If he doesn't find the seller, what
will happen next?
MOVE across the TABLES, past a middle-aged AMERICAN COUPLE, to TWO
TURKISH PLAINCLOTHESMEN watching him closely. They look evident. TWO
HIPPIES make a wide berth around them.

17

HIPPIES (OFF)
(in passing, low)
Hey Janet, why don't you go sell
'em some dope.
MOVE ON to another TABLE where TWO MORE PLAINCLOTHESMEN sit, equally evident, watching BILLY.
TEX sits in his car, in the distance, casually glancing at a newspaper.
BILLY's eyes rove.
INTERIOR PUDDING SHOPPE Large. Many tables. Stairs. A back exit.
ANOTHER GYPSY BOY leads a huge PINK PIG leashed with a wooden sign around its neck proclaiming "Pig" in Turkish.
Various TURKS point the pig out, laughing at it, some disgusted by it, making faces and gestures: "Go way, go way! "Ayip!" The PIG moves past BILLY, who shifts his gaze to:
POV - CABDRIVER #1 lingering at the curb. PAN to CABDRIVER
#2 PAN to CABDRIVER #3. PAN BACK to #1 and again to #2 indicating no real fix on identity.
BILLY tense now, knowing this is the chance he must take, nods with his head, pointing at CABDRIVER #2, off.
THE PLAINCLOTHESMEN move out towards CABDRIVER #2.
BILLY tentatively rises, as if to join them, but moves slyly towards the interior of the cafe.
PLAINCLOTHESMEN move in roughly on a surprised CABDRIVER
#2 who begins to protest LOUDLY (AD LIB).
BILLY moves through the INTERIOR of the PUDDING SHOPPE, past the tables, past the stairs, towards the back of the shop, at a normal.to attract attention.
A PLAINCLOTHESMAN looks around, sees he is gone. Tells the others (AD LIB) They spread out looking, abandoning the
CABDRIVER #2 who spits and curses them (AD LIB).
BILLY, with one backward glance, now eases out the BACK
DOOR, into a bilious sunlight, onto a STREET. Pause.
A HAND with GUN moves into FRAME pointing a six-inch barrel right at his temple.
BILLY freezes, moving just his eyes to:
TEX looking down at him calm, merciless.

TEX
You seem like a nice enough kid to me Billy, but try it and I'll blow your fucking brains out.
BILLY - the sense of betrayal in his eyes.
ESTABLISH PRISON - OVERHEAD ANGLE. A large and Byzantine structure suggesting the 15th Century Sultan's Janissary
Barracks. Irregular crescent various wings; a MOSQUE inside the prison. The possibly a shapes to the sense of an endless a decorative an equally in a city, labyrinth built by some mad Arab architect to suit purpose and now, in the 20th

18

Century, transformed by mad Turkish bureaucracy into a prison. It should be preferably made to look like Istanbul.

Faint background atonal Turkish CHANTING. Evening Muslim prayer."Allah wakbah, Allah wakbah..." on and on, suggesting to us fear rather than praise.

BILLY VOICE

Dear Mom and Dad. This is the hardest letter I've ever had to write. know the confusion and the pain it will cause you. And the disappointment...

BILLY - his scalp being shaved off by a prison BARBER in an un-specified ANTI-CHAMBER, His eyes are staring dead ahead.

BILLY VOICE

(continuous)

I really thought knew what I was doing with my life. I'd hoped somehow to get out of this quickly so that you'd never know about it.

But that just isn't possible now.

I don't know what's going to happen.

But what can I say to you? Will

'I'm sorry' make a difference?

Will it ease the pain, the shame you must be feeling? Forgive me...Please...

BILLY is now completely BALD, SOUND SHARP OVER:

CUT:

A CELL DOOR SLIDING OPEN. BILLY steps in, bewildered.

ZIAT VOICE (OFF)

Git!

The cell is dark, almost black, an overpowering stench; a small grey metal bunk is bolted to the floor with a lumpy mattress. BILLY turns, looking back at the man staring at him from the door.

ZIAT is quickly summing up Billy's character. This is his craft.He is a prisoner and trustee. sinister man whose one motivation in life is the accumulation of money, in the pursuit of which he has acquired an ugly purplish SCAR running the width of his throat, various other facial SCARS; and one blind milky white EYE. He's stocky and strong -- about five ten, with bushy eyebrows, brown cigarette teeth, big dirty nails, repulsively in need of a bath. What's surprising is that he is no more than thirty years old looks and behaves like sixty. The personification of the denaturalization of a man. Time, body, mind - all of them warped.

BILLY, not yet attuned to his nature, only repulsed, is still wearing his own clothes and makes a shivering gesture, enunciating very clearly, hoping he will understand.

BILLY

Cold. Very cold. Can I get blanket?

Blanket?

(makes a gesture of a blanket wrapped around him)

19

ZIAT smiles, showing his stained teeth, and starts to slide shut the cell door on its ROLLER.

ZIAT
(in English)
Mo sell...Too late. Tomorrow...
A cobra smile flashes, as the cell door bangs shut.

ZIAT
(through the bars)
You be here tomorrow. "Ayi
Gedjaler"("good night")
Goes.
BILLY walks around the cell, hugging himself for warmth.

VOICE (OFF)
Pssst!
BILLY stops, goes to the edge of the cell.
A BONY BARE ARM motions from the bars of the cell next to his. We never see the face but hear a thick ITALIAN ACCENT, hoarse and cracked.

VOICE (OFF)
(Whispering)
Your cell, no key. Open...!
Blanket. Three cell down. You get me one. Take...
Extends a stick with a big nail pounded into the end, twisted over to form a hook.
BILLY takes it. Hesitates.

VOICE (OFF)
Ziat go for night. Go!
BILLY cautiously slides the cell door open, amazed that it's been left open. Nothing makes any sense to him in this labyrinth
ANOTHER ANGLE - BILLY steps out into a WALKWAY. A bare bulb overhead casts light. He glides past the three cells, seemingly empty. Finds the cell with blankets, sheets, towels and various supplies stacked inside. But it's locked. He slips the stick in between the bars and stretching, hooks the first blanket.
BILLY asleep with the blankets pulled up to his chin.
Suddenly DIRTY HANDS reach into frame and rip the blanket off. WIDEN TO:

ZIAT
(tugging the sheet, growls)
Brack!...Brack!
Then SLAPS at BILLY. BILLY ducks away. Encouraged, ZIAT steps up closer to him, sticks his fingers in his chest screaming.

ZIAT

You, goddamn you, give me sheet.

Give me!

And feints as if to hit BILLY again. BILLY reacts to defend himself, pushing ZIAT off and jumping out of the bunk.

ZIAT, Enraged by the shove, comes back at BILLY, screaming, arms flailing like a bear to pummel him, but BILLY, not understanding the Turkish bluster in his mannerisms, meets him with a sharp right FIST into the front of his face.

ZIAT staggers back, startled into silence; he has misjudged this kid.

BILLY waits, ready for the fight in the defensive position.

The guy is bigger than himself. ZIAT, however, now feels the blood from his mouth and nose and freaks out, running out of the cell SCREAMING at the top of his lungs as if he's dying.

CUT:

BILLY is blindfolded, stumbling down stone steps pushed by a GUARD, into a dungeon-like basement room. THE PUNISHMENT

CELLS.

CUT:

THE GUARD removes the blindfold. BILLY, adjusting to the light, stares around. The cell is spartan, with a series of pulleys and primitive bondage devices hanging from the cobwebbed ceiling.A DOOR opens and:

HAMIDOU STEPS in, lowering his head to get through the door.Chief of the guards. A clean uniform. Four stripes.

The only guard to carry a holstered gun. very frightening man. He is about six two, two forty, and muscular, and moves lightly like a fighter on his feet. His skull is bullet-shaped and completely shaven like Billy's, Enhancing this effect, he has no eyebrows, and his pale blue eyes

(suggesting a trace of Indo-European stock in his ancestry) are set deep in his skull somewhat like turtle eyes, giving nothing away. His nose is a beak of skin his neck broad, his mouth a small crescent that moves as lightly as his feet between anger and amusement. He approaches BILLY, looks into his eyes, drawing out the moment for himself, enjoying the tension and the fear he instils in others.

BILLY meets his eyes respectfully, then realizing this is perhaps not the thing do to, looks away. But, fascinated by the man's features beyond his self-control, he looks back.

HAMIDOU, amused by eye actions, smiles thinly. The sort of smile that could imply friendship such is its hint of charm.

HAMIDOU
(to one of the guards)
Name?

GUARD
(checking a clipboard)
Vilyum Hi-yes

HAMIDOU
(looking at BILLY, repeating it)
Vilyum Hi-yes...
And slowly his hand moves up to caress the edge of his hairless upper lip. An erotic gesture in Turkey.

HAMIDOU
Vilyum Hi-yes
"Its in my memory locked." He slowly extends his right arm stiff out to his side.
BILLY watches, fascinated.
HAMIDOU lets the arm linger; then:
SMASHES BILLY across the face with an open palm. BILLY shoots back: and smashes against the wall just from the force of one blow. Stunned.
HAMIDOU advances, taking a wooden CLUB (FALUKA STICK) about feet three long and three inches wide from a GUARD.
BILLY scared, emphasizing the words, trying to make himself understood.

BILLY
It was cold. Cold! I get blanket.
Blanket! Cold!

THWACK!
BILLY'S LEG BUCKLES, where the faluka stick has just smashed him behind the kneecap. He SCREAMS going down.
BILLY looks up from the floor:
HAMIDOU with his club in hand.

HAMIDOU
(In some sort of
English, smiles)
No do. No do.
Raises the club.
BILLY tries to block it with his hand, and the CLUB smashes his thumb. SCREAM.

SHARP CUT:
BILLY is hoisted upside-down in his UNDERPANTS ONLY with thick rope tied about his ankles, the legs spread - onto a
PULLEY suspended from the ceiling. He is yanked upwards, then lowered slightly, his head and backs of shoulders banging against the stone floor.
THE PULLEY is LOCKED into place. (LOUD SOUND)
BILLY has this surprised look on his face still, through the tears. What's happening?
Hamidou motions the GUARDS out of the room (AD LIB). Turns back to BILLY, raises his club.
BRINGS IT DOWN FORCE on the soles of BILLY'S BARE FEET.
SCREAM. He cocks the club again.
BILLY twists To avoid The blow

CLUB catches him On The ANKLEBONE
BILLY SCREAMs louder than ever as we hear The SOUND of wood On bone. Whimpering SOUNDS follow.
BILLY looking through teary eyes, sure now that he is going to be killed. The CLUB - OFF - smacks sole skin with the same force as the first blow. No let up.

CUT:
BILLY still in the same position, vomits all over himself.
HAMIDOU SPINS the PULLEY to a new position bringing:
BILLY into a steeper, more vertical position. He is on the verge of fainting, bleary-eyed, looking as:
HAMIDOU moves around in between his legs. Doing something indistinct with the stick between his legs, then dropping the stick. Then, with this bizarrely excited expression on his hairless face, he begins to undo his own pants. But, for Billy, it all BLURS OUT TO:
JAPANESE SILK SCREEN depicting a fat jovial Buddhist monk, fishing placidly by a stream. Then moves to soap carvings of chess pieces Then a bed-sheet hung as a curtain with astrological symbols paint; on it. SOUND OFF, of a blaring radio. Atonal TURKISH MUSIC.

VOICE
(close, intense)
Hey man, he's gotta walk, or his feet gonna swell up worse.

2ND VOICE
(softer, sonorous,
Swedish accent)
We take him down to courtyard...
Then: ERICH - a gentle long bird's face. Long whitish-blond- hair, Swedish, well above six feet, 25.
Another FACE moves into view JIMMY BELL, American, 23 fiery eyes, black hair and moustache, intense, strong.

BELL
Smoke this rocket, it'll cool the pain.
ANOTHER ANGLE - BELL puts a huge cone-shaped JOINT with aluminium foil filter into BILLY'S LIPS. He hardly knows what it is, Puffing weakly. Though dehydrated and his face white without color, he has no facial markings.

BELL
You gotta walk around some man, or your feet gonna swell up something bad...
BILLY looks down at
HIS FEET Bloated black and blue with inflamed red points in various spots. A vicious bruise on his anklebone. ERICH is running a cold rag from a basin of water over them, his fingers tender.

BELL (OVER)
You've been out for days man, talking all kinds of shit. Come on, we'll walk you down to the courtyard.
BELL eases BILLY up from the bed, as ERICH puts a pair of clip-clops on his feet.

ERICH
Okay?
BILLY nods. They rise together, bracing his shoulder.
BILLY adjusting to the sensation of standing.

ERICH
How's it feel?

BILLY
(dizzy)
About as good as it looks.

BELL
Getchmis olsun

BILLY
Getchmis...?

BELL
Olsun - "May it pass quickly." I'm
Bell, Jimmy Bell. This is Erich something Swedish.

ERICH
(smiling)
Just Erich.

BILLY
I'm Billy Hayes... At least I used to be.
Looks around.
A DORMITORY TYPE ROOM with 24 bunk beds set head to head in horizontal fashion, cramped and with minimal privacy. A narrow WALKWAY leading towards a TOILET AREA and STAIRCASE.

BILLY
Looks like a cheap hotel.

BELL
Yeah... Only the room service is lousy. Come on, let me show you the tennis courts.
Helps him with ERICH to take the first steps.
THE COURTYARD. The THREE of them emerge in a thin AFTERNOON sun, Billy now disengaging and hobbling on his own power.

ERICH
(watching Billy limp)
Feeling all right?

BILLY
(still groggy)
Yeah. That guy who beat me?
(stops, slightly puzzled)
I feel stoned.

BELL
(grins, interjects)
'Figgers.

BILLY
(vague, going on)
...He had a bald skull and...

BELL
Hamidou. Chief of the Guards.
Don't fuck with him. He almost killed an Italian dude couple months ago. Bad news.
He try anything with you?
BILLY glances at him, understanding. Pause.

BILLY
No... I don't remember.
Glances at ERICH.

BELL
With these fucking Turks, soon as the light goes out... I keep one hand on their feet and
their feet better not grow. You'll meet Max.
He got raped something bad down in
Section 13. That's the pits.

THE COURTYARD
VARIOUS ANGLES The yard is 30 by 50 paces with a wall 20 feet high. Cigarette
butts, orange peels crumpled news- papers, rocks, sticks, broken glass litter the place.
No guards are on the walls; the only GUARDS are unarmed inanimate lumps of
boredom who look as helpless as the prisoners with whom they intermingle; they have
raggedy olive green uniforms and worn boots (they make $1 a month, augmented by
bribes). On one side of the yard is a 2-story
ROGUS (cellblock) with barred windows from which Billy and his two companions
have just emerged. On the other side of the yard is another 2-story KOGUS (the
children's kogus).

25

The COURTYARD is colorful, almost like a bazaar, about 8O people in it - groups of exotically dressed AFRICANS,
AFGHANS, ARABS, MALAYSIANS, EUROPEANS, and predominantly
TURKS pacing back and forth talking in little circles, hawking wares, trading illegal currencies.
Screaming Turkish STREET URCHINS 10-14 years old, share the space playing soccer and volleyball with a surprising viciousness, continually hitting each other and cursing. A bunch of them vehemently lay bets on the soccer game.
Other aspects of the prison which should become evident:
1) NOISE - continuous, Loud. Radios, Turkish music, screaming, shouting. 2) CATS - all kinds, some of them pets, some stray, tolerated because they kill the rats. 3)
THE PRISONERS all wear their own clothing; the foreigners preferring jeans, clip-clops, sneakers, Sweat suits. 4)
THE HEADS of only the new prisoners are shaved, then allowed to grow back. 5)
MANY PRISONERS have physical disabilities.
Carbuncles on the back from wet mattresses. Boils on the lymph glands around the neck, buttocks, under-arms, sometimes SO painful the victim walks with his arms up in the air. Arthritic in the knees, hips, ankles. Fungus on the feet. Many limp.
ANOTHER ANGLE - THE PRISONERS glance at BILLY as he walks, noting the beating he has taken and sizing him up, then going on with their business.

BILLY
The kids? Why are they...

BELL
(snorts)
Little fuckers are thieves, rapists, pickpockets, murderers, you name it - they do it. Don't trust any of 'em...
BELL's eyes follow a knot of KIDS to:
ZIAT has a window open on the FIRST FLOOR KOGUS and is selling little cups of tea to the kids from inside where he works a GAS STOVE. The kids push and punch each other to get the tea faster.

BELL (OVER)
...They tell Ziat everything. He's the squeal round here. Goes all over the prison. Sells watered- down tea, blankets, hash, black money, nembutols --anything for a buck...
ZIAT leaves the stove in the hands of an ASSISTANT and moves down the window to a particularly gaudy AFGHANI a fierce hawk-faced old man with a chunk of his ear missing.
He wears a colorful flowing robe, various scarves, turban, trinkets, rings, baggy pants, and pointed curved shoes, and makes emphatic violent gestures at ZIAT with his mutilated THREE FINGERS. ZIAT Seems to speak something of his language and bargains back.

BELL
(continuous)

He was an informer on the outside but he tried to screw the cops out of 60 kilos of opium. Watch him, he's a fox.

BILLY says nothing to them about the Ziat incident, sizing him up for himself.

THE AFGHANI having concluded the deal with ZIAT reaches deep into his layers of clothing around his crotch and pulls out several scrofulous $10 bills which discreetly takes in exchange for a thick wad of Turkish currency, his eyes moving around, stopping on BILLY. A hooded look.

BELL (OVER)
Whatcha' in for, smuggling? Rash?
BILLY turning his eyes away from ZIAT

BILLY
Yeah.

BELL
(shaking his head)
History, man, history. How much?

BILLY
Two kilos.

BELL
Where?

BILLY
The airport. Trying to get on the plane for the States.

BELL
(whistling a kind of punctuation)
Could be ten or fifteen. Maybe even twenty.

BILLY
(tensing)
Twenty months?

BELL
Twenty fucking YEARS, man - YEARS!
I figger ten at the least.
BILLY stunned.

BILLY
(soft)
Years?

BELL

Yeah, what do you think this is, the good USA? This is Turkey, man...
(laughs bitterly))
It's a fucking accident here if you're innocent. And anyway...
...ain't nobody who's innocent.
ANOTHER ANGLE - all the color and breath seems to have gone from BILLY.

ERICH
(his English is halting but has a calming effect)
Don't pay too much attention, anything is possible in Turkey.
You might get bail.
BELL snorts, amused, kicking the SOCCER BALL away hard as it dribbles towards them.

ERICH
...If you make bail, you're free.
You can get a fake passport or sneak across the border to Greece.
The Greeks hate the Turks so much they never send you back. The Turks know it. They just keep the bail. money.

BELL
Sure, keep dreaming and see where that gets you... like Max, up in the head, you know...
(makes a crazy signal towards the head)
You gonna eat a lot more fasoulia beans, Billy baby, 'fore you taste a hamburger 'gain cause you broke the law man, and you got caught...
(grins)
And that... is history.

ERICH
The law is sometimes wrong.

BELL
(eyes feverish)
The Law is never wrong, asshole.
The Law is!
And stalks away, disgusted. A deep anger inside him. ERICH looks at BILLY who is quiet; by way of apology.

ERICH
New people sometimes get on his nerves.

BILLY
(lifeless)
What did he do?

ERIC
He was caught steeling from a

28

Mosque. That's heavy here. He got 30 years.

BILLY
Thirty years?

ERICH
Jimmy has more balls than brains.
He didn't tell his parents he was in jail for a year and a half. He says he got himself in and now he's going to get himself out.
He shakes his head, looking at:
BELL him across the courtyard huddling with a cigarette, bartering angrily. a raggedy GUARD giving him a cigarette, bartering angrily.
BILLY and ERICH.

BILLY
And you?

ERICH
Hashish. Ninety percent of the foreigners are in for hashish.
They walk.

BILLY
What they give you?

ERICH
(passive)
Twelve years.
Billy stops.

BILLY
How much did you have?

ERICH
A hundred grams.

BILLY
(appalled)
It's not fair!
Even ERICH has to smile now.

ERICH
There is no fair in Turkey, Billy.
It's all "sula-bula" like this, like that. An Italian hippie had a car accident and a Turk was killed.
SO, they threw him in here for six months...

BILLY
That doesn't seem so bad.

ERICH
But he was eating lunch a mile away when the Turk smashed into killed himself.

BILLY
He wasn't even in the car?

ERICH
(shakes his head)
Aslan, there...
(points)
ASLAN - a young big fat heavily moustached Turk, wearing a black silk double-breasted business suit, grotesque cuff- links, heavily pomaded hair, is huddling in a section of the YARD with FIVE other grinning GANGSTER TYPES, all in suits.

ERICH (OVER)
Killed a guy. But his father's a big gangster on the docks. A
"Kapidiye." He'll stay in... twelve months no more, and get parole. In
Turkey, murder is manly - "erkek".
ERICH Glances back at BILLY

ERICH
You just got to get yourself a good lawyer. And some money...
Talk to Max. He's been in the longest.

BILLY
How long?

ERICH
Seven years...

CUT:
MAX - "Eskilet" (skeleton). British, tall, straggly long hair with wire spectacles set crookedly over his nose. An earing in one ear. The far away eyes of an international junkie, preoccupied and uninterested in small talk. Tough in his skinny way, like apiece of old dried leather.
He occupies with his YOUNG STRIPED CAT a bunk in the far corner of the SECOND FLOOR KOGUS - in the process of shooting himself up with "Gastro" a smelly brown liquid stomach medicine. No one is in the vicinity except

ANOTHER ANGLE
ERICH and BILLY who watches repelled as MAX fumbles with a piece of twine tied around his arm in a tourniquet, searching for an unused spot amid dirty infected track marks. PLUNGES the needle in, pumping in the black gunk.

Glances at BILLY.

MAX
(smiles)
Gastro. Stomach medicine. Has codeine in it... Best can do
Pulls out the needle, loosens the tourniquet. His eyes take on a far away stare.

ERICH
Lawyers?

MAX
Yeah... there's no straight lawyers in Turkey... They're all bent bent as hairpins...
Gives a spoon with a taste of the black residue to:
HIS CAT who is full of spunk, and tries to catch Max's

HAND.
He looks at BILLY, not remembering him.

ERICH
His name?

MAX
Who?

ERICH
The lawyer?
MAX is beginning to go. He sits on his bunk.

MAX
What lawyer?

ERICH
Who got the Frenchman out?

MAX
Oh Yesil... Yesil's his name but
I...don't know anything...
'bout...Yesil...
ANOTHER ANGLE - MAX'S head begins to bob back and forth.Focuses on BILLY.

MAX
Best way is get your ass out... any... way... you can...

BILLY
What do you mean?

MAX
Get the... midnight... express.

BILLY
What's that?
MAX smiles from faraway like a Cheshire cat and his head drops forward onto his knees, nodding off.

CUT:
HAMIDOU, swinging his falaka stick rhythmically against his leg and that calm killer look on his face, leads an uneasy BILLY down a MAIN WALKWAY with a roof overhead; we gather that the prison contains several separate wings.
ADMINISTRATIVE BUILDING - HAMIDOU glances back at BILLY, indicates with his stick "come here" and opens an office door.
BILLY, still bewildered, his bruised feet almost back to normal, limps in warily eyeing HAMIDOU who follows.
NECDIT YESIL, the lawyer, fleshy, grinning, thin black hair heavily greased, sits at a conference table. Standing adjacent is STANLEY DAVIS, the U.S. Consul - eyeglasses, striped tie, neat summer suit with stripes, trimmed hair, ivy league look, his eyes moving from Billy to:
OLDER MAN, late 50's white hair, blue-eyed New York
Irishman.A suburban insurance agent, rumpled suit, an anxious look on his face. Moving towards BILLY fast:

FATHER
Billy!
FATHER AND SON embrace; the father's left hand grabbing
Billy's arm tightly as if never to let go.

BILLY
Dad!
HAMIDOU looks on, intrigued by the Father and Son; leaves silently, closing the door.
FATHER looks into his son's eyes, his own eyes moistening.
He looks tired, pain all over his face.
BILLY looks down.

BILLY
Dad...I'm...

ANOTHER ANGLE
FATHER
(voice quivering)
...Don't worry about it.
(managing a smile)
I can punch you in the nose later.
Right now we've got to get you out of here. You all right?

32

BILLY
(eyes moistening)
Yeah. How's Mom?

FATHER
Bad. She couldn't make the trip.
You know Her boy...
(breaks off)
Susan told us before we got your letter. She's fine; she's trying to get the money to come back and see you, but...

BILLY
No, don't let her! I'll... How about Peg? Robbie?

FATHER
Same. None of the neighbors know.
We told them you were in a hospital in Europe. Oh... this is Stanley Davis. He's the American Consul here... And Necdit Yesil, the lawyer you wanted...

ANOTHER ANGLE
DAVIS
(shaking hands)
Hello, Billy.

BILLY
Hello.
The professional smile from the Consul, but in the handshake and the eye contact, BILLY is cool. The unanswered question:
Where were you before my father arrived?

DAVIS
I want you to know we're going to do everything, in our power to get you out as soon as possible. Believe me.

BILLY
Thank you.

ANOTHER ANGLE
YESIL moves forward. unctuous. bubbling with high spirits, profusely shaking BILLY's hand, exuding confidence in fractured English,

YESIL
Vilyum, I am Necdit Yesil.

BILLY

Mr. Yesil.

YESIL
I know exactly what you feel but you must not worry, we are acting immediately, we get the right court, the right judge, I arrange everything - just right. And I think we get you bail. If very bad, maybe twenty month sentence...
But I think we get you bail...
Pause, BILLY looks at him wondering how to take him in.

YESIL
(reassuringly)
You know I have lectured at the
University of Maryland in your country? Also University Michigan
Very nice country. We both go back.
(smiles)

BILLY
(trying to concentrate)
If I get bail, Mister Yesil, they say it's easy to cross the border into Greece?

FATHER
(pacing up, hungry)
Right! That's what we're shooting for. Mister Davis and have been in contact with the State
Department, but right now relations with the Turks aren't too good,
Nixon's upset the hell out of them.
Our best bet's... right here.

BILLY
Dad...
(pauses, glances at
Davis and Yesil, embarrassed)
I'll pay you back for all this, I
Promise.

ANOTHER ANGLE
FATHER
Don't worry about it. Right now money doesn't count. Okay?
A pause. YESIL Shifts, Throats are cleared. BILLY moves to sit down, limping faintly; he is wearing sneakers and the bruises don't show.

FATHER
Where'd you get that limp?

BILLY
(not wanting to alarm him)

34

Nothing. Just twisted my ankle.
Sits down at the conference TABLE.

BILLY
Where you staying, Dad?

FATHER
(pulls up a seat next to Billy)
The Hilton.

BILLY
How do you like it? Istanbul?

FATHER
Well, it's an interesting place...
(lowers his voice, a hint of a smile)
Tell you the truth, I think the food is lousy. The crap they sell in these little restaurants.
I went out to eat in one of them last night, and I had to run to the damn toilet... You
shoulda' seen the toilet.
BILLY laughs.

BILLY
You mean you got toilets?
FATHER is happy to see his son laugh.

FATHER
Yeah, with real toilet paper - and you don't have to use both sides.
BILLY laughs again.

FATHER
So now I'm eating at the Hilton every night.
BILLY smiles. A pause. A worried look returns to the
Father's face

FATHER
Why'd you do it, Billy?

BILLY
For the money...
(Looks away))

FATHER
(sighs)
I know you kids smoke that stuff, and we drink booze, but taking it across a border - it
was stupid,
Billy. Stupid.

35

BILLY

I know.

Glances at DAVIS, YESIL back to his father, his voice beginning to tremble, ashamed of himself for letting it show.

BILLY

Dad get me out of here.

ANOTHER ANGLE. The FATHER understands the desperation in his voice, puts his hand on his son's.

FATHER I promise you, Billy. Just sit tight and don't..

DON'T do anything stupid. Let me work with Mr. Yesil and

Mr. Davis. We'll get you out... Okay? Billy, okay?

All the assurance of the world is written in this kindly

Irishman's face.

BILLY feels it.

BILLY being led by TWO GUARDS down a huge arched CORRIDOR in the COURTROOM BUILDING.

BILLY

Okay.

CUT:

PROSECUTOR VOICE (OVER)

THE world is now looking at Turkey.

We are called the Heroin Supplier of the world. Stories about us are in newspapers and on television every day all around the world.

The time has come, your Honor, to alter this image before we find ourselves isolated and morally ostracized by the rest of the human race...

THE COURTROOM - monolithic, frightening, immense with cross- currents of greenish light from the enormous windows.

People seem insignificant.

THE PROSECUTOR, wearing dark green glasses, continues, scowling, gesturing profusely at:

BILLY in the PRISONERS DOCK, baroque design, isolated.

Doesn't understand a thing, Erich's extra-large blue pin- striped suit makes him look rather absurd.

HIS FATHER, CONSUL DAVIS, YESIL and ANOTHER LAWYER are seated together at the defence table conferring in low tones with each other. YESIL looks over at BILLY with a big reassuring grin, nods his head - nothing to worry about.

TURKISH GIRL from the Press with a yellow legal pad, makes notes in the Spectator Gallery. Her legs flare out from a short skirt.

BILLY pries his eyes away to:

PROSECUTOR continuing in front of the THREE JUDGES high on an Alice in Wonderland podium wearing long black robes with scarlet collars. One of the Judges is bald, the other has his eyes closed, could be asleep. The CHIEF JUDGE in the middle has a sagging somewhat kindly face and short grey hair. A YOUNG MAN below the podium, is clacking at an ancient typewriter on a small table.

PROSECUTOR VOICE (OVER)
(continuous)
...We must alter this image by punishing only our own drug smugglers-but by handing out foreigners who infest our culture with their depravity ungodly and behavior. We must start now - by sentencing this American, Vilyum
Hi-yes, to the maximum sentence for smuggling, to be held up to the light of the world as an example of Turkish justice and its intention to halt the drug trade once and for all..
.I ask the Court therefore to sentence Vilyum Hi-yes to Life
Imprisonment.
He sits, staring malignantly at BILLY.
THE JUDGES rise.

JUDGE
Thank you, Prosecutor. The Court will now recess to consider its verdict.
The JUDGES exit.
ANOTHER ANGLE, General commotion in the courtroom as people move about. The FATHER and DAVIS and the OTHER LAWYER consult among themselves, the FATHER vigorously nodding his head. YESIL approaches BILLY.
BILLY leans forward anxiously in the dock.

BILLY
What'd the Prosecutor say?

YESIL
(hurried)
It's not important, just technical things. We make our case. You were very good, you spoke well.
The Judge like you. It look good.
Don't worry.

BILLY
(pressing)
Did you ask for bail?
But YESIL is called over by the other LAWYER and hurries off. A SOLDIER comes over and sits BILLY down.

CUT:
THE CHIEF JUDGE puts on his glasses, stands to read the verdict.
YESIL, standing with the OTHERS, motions BILLY to rise.
BILLY rises, tense.
FATHER looks over at him, manages a reassuring smile.
JUDGE continuing, after preliminaries:

37

JUDGE
The Defendant has been found guilty by the Court of the illegal possession of Hashish...
PROSECUTOR, his expression souring, makes a gesture of defeat. We wanted a conviction for smuggling, not possession.
BILLY, not understanding sees the Prosecutor's gesture, and a hint of hope crosses his expression.
JUDGE puts the paper away, looks at BILLY directly.

JUDGE
...Therefore. this court sentences you, Vilyum Hi-yes to be imprisoned at Sagamilcar Prison for a term of four years and two months. This
Case is now closed.
BILLY looking at the JUDGE doesn't understand. Thinks he might be free. But suddenly TWO SOLDIERS move in, and start chaining his hands together. He is bewildered, looking at:
YESIL hastily conferring with Billy's FATHER, more concerned about making a good impression with him than with Billy.

YESILF
Four years, two months. It's good.

FATHER
(stunned)
Four years!

YESIL
(quickly)
We appeal it.
BILLY watching this, a lost look.
FATHER is too shocked to do anything but look at YESIL who continues on:

YESIL
You will see, he will have maybe one year taken off this sentence for good behaviour. Remember, it is only for possession; the prosecutor wanted life sentence for smuggling...
(a smile)
To be honest Mr. Hayes, it is a great victory!
BILLY is forcibly removed from the DOCK - in chains.

CUT:
THE FATHER, in the same CONFERENCE ROOM,

FATHER
(embarrassed)

...With good time Billy it works out to about 3 years... then there's the appeal. Yesil, Davis, they're all working for you We're going to try to make a deal to get you transferred to a Stateside prison.

And Davis thinks there might be a political amnesty any month...

Stops. Knows it sounds bad.

BILLY looks down.

FATHER
Look - I know it sounds tough,
Billy, but we're gonna get you out...
FATHER grips BILLY by the arm hard.

FATHER
...I promise you, but I don't want you to get stupid again. Pull anything. They can play with your sentence.
BILLY nods, acquiescent.

FATTIER
(his voice starting to crack)
I'm putting $500 in the bank for you. Anything you need you write...
BILLY nods. His FATHER points to a stack of ITEMS on the conference table, picks up a cigarette carton.

FATHER
There's food, candy, writing paper, soap, books...
(his eyes start to water)
...cigarettes, soap, tooth-brush, there's... Jesus!
(cracks, throws down the cigarette carton)
I been writing insurance policies on people for thirty goddamn years...
(laughs and cries at the same time)
And now I gotta see my own son...Jesus! Jesus! If I could be where you are Billy, I'd be there...
Goddamn Jesus! These bastards.
HUGS HIS SON BILLY is on the verge of tears.

BILLY
DAD!
FATHER
Oh Jesus!
(sobbing)
HAMIDOU enters the room. A morbid curiosity in his expression about this show of grief. Watches a few moments, then indicating the visit is over, he taps his falaka stick lightly a few times on the hollow door. THWACK! THWACK!
FATHER breaks the embrace with BILLY, tears streaking his cheeks. Silently indicates for him to "Go, go Fast."
BILLY goes, past HAMIDOU

FATHER shaking his finger at HAMIDOU

FATHER
You take good care of my boy, you hear, or I'll have your fucking head, you Turkish bastard!
It sputters out of his mouth, senseless to:
HAMIDOU who closes the door. He has an angry glint in his eye.

CUT:
BILLY lies on his bunk at night deeply depressed, paler.
Candlelight flutters softly against the stone walls. A
PHOTO of SUSAN taken outdoors with a mountain range in the background, is on his wall with various SOAP CARVINGS of little chess piece she has designed.
In the distance, very faintly coming upwards into our sound consciousness we hear a TRAIN WHISTLING in the night, on an old railroad track bypassing the prison walls. Two whistles. Chugging. Then passing off. The Midnight Express.

BILLY'S VOICE
Dear Susan. 1970 has now passed into 1971. You can drift in here and never know you're gone. You can fade so far out and you don't know where you are anymore or where anything else is...
The CAMERA DRIFTS around the SECOND STORY KOGUS revealing the sleepers: ERICH, BELL, MAX...

BILLY'S VOICE
(continuous)
I find loneliness is a physical pain which hurts all over; you can't isolate it in one part of your body. I so much need your softness, your strength. I have your letters. They charge me, give me courage.News about amnesty and getting out - tangled, complicated...
The CAMERA LINGERS on ZIAT in a far corner of the Kogus, top bunk, against a wall. Never secure, he shuffles in his sleep.

VOICE
...I feel myself drifting more heavily into smoking hashish. The haze helps the time pass. Also I do soap carvings. Erich taught me. And I have been learning Turkish because it helps me to deal with the guards and the prisoners. I'm trying hard to maintain some sort of schedule to my life, but sometimes it seems like I'm just trying in order to try...
ZIAT is evidently awake he pulls his RADIO over into the bed, and peering around to make sure no one is watching, here moves the screws from the back of it, pulls off the cover and puts in a sheaf of large denomination GERMAN
MARKS: inside we briefly glimpse a wad of different-colored
CURRENCIES stacked with rubber bands.

CUT:

COURTYARD. Volleyball game in progress. ERICH is tall and plays with dexterous grace. BILLY is fast, agile. BELL is muscular, intense, his hits power-packed.

BILLY'S VOICE
(continuous)
... In the daytimes we sometimes play volleyball against the big
Turkish gangsters...
THE THREE they play against are hilarious looking in this context, moving like big clumsy bears, waving their arms and screaming at each other, disorganized. Ever conscious of fashion, they have their jackets and vests off but play in their Elvis Presley shirts rolled up at the sleeves, shiny slacks, black pointed pumps. The boys wear shorts and sneakers. On the sidelines we see a group of PRISONERS laying bets and shouting encouragement.
BILLY leaps up for a ball close to the net and as the
TURKISH OPPONENT backs off, he dinks the ball in just over the net; the Turk SCREAMS his teammates scream at him.

CUT:
BELL goes up for another ball close to the net and really
SMASHES it with all his might, and:
BALL bangs right into the eye of a TURK who flails his arms and SCREAMS with pain, very theatrical.

CUT:
THE SAME TURK now swaggers around the COURTYARD, wearing sunglasses so no one will see his black eye.

BILLY'S VOICE
...To the Turks all foreigners are
"ayip" - unclean, dirty. We don't shave our under-arms or around our crotch...
BELL across the pointyard grins at him and points him out to BILLY, and ERICH.

BILLY VOICE
(continuous)
Even the yoga I sometimes do is
"ayip" - too suggestive...
THE TURK scowls back at BELL, huddles menacingly with another TURK.

BILLY'S VOICE
(continuous)
And you're never supposed to eat with your left hand. You know why?
Because that's what they use to wipe their asses with instead of toilet paper. And yet they hate pigs. There are no pigs in Turkey.
They're considered dirty...
BELL, smirking at the Turk, turns and walks away.

BILLY VOICE

(continuous)

So is homosexuality. That's a big crime here but most of them do it every chance they get. There are about a thousand things that are

"ayip". But they're really so hypocritical, like children breaking the rules. For instance...

Suddenly a CRY OFF and:

THE TURK runs up, pulling a sharp SHIV from his pants, and using the cloth as a handle he repeatedly STABS BELL in the ass and backs of his thighs. One, two, three, four, five QUICK STABS, like a cook hammering veal. In spite of its violence, the action seems like slapstick.

BELL tumbles to the ground, crying out.

THE TURK stashes the shiv and disappears among his FRIENDS, his honor restored.

BILLY and ERICH run over to help BELL who is obviously more in pain than in danger.

BILLY VOICE

(continuous)

...You can stab or shoot some body the but not above the waist because that's intent to kill. So everybody runs around stabbing everyone else in the ass. That's what they call 'Turkish revenge'. There's also a lot of "Baksheesh" that's a favorite

Turkish word for bribery...

LONG SHOT - HAMIDOU and ASLAN the young fat Turkish gangster pointed out previously by Erich, are taking tea together in the FIRST STORY KOGUS alone except for ZIATR and

Hamidou's two FAT SONS, 7 and 8 years old, both dressed in little suits listening politely as Hamidou gestures to them, in couched terms. The voices are distant and, after a few beats, UNDER BILLY'S VOICE:

HAMIDOU

Unfortunately my youngest son Arief is having problems with his teeth; he needs braces, but dentists are so expensive these days

ASLAN

(patting Arief on the head)

Poor kid... You know I have a friend, a very good friend; he's a dentist; maybe he could get you some braces at a... reasonable price.

HAMIDOU

(protesting with his hands, shaking his head))

Oh, no...it's out of the question...wouldn't want to ask your friend...

ASLAN

Yes. Please! As a favour... I insist

They go on, each protesting.

BILLY VOICE

(continuous)

Hamidou hints that he needs new braces for one of his sons. Aslan of course has a friend who's a dentist. They bullshit for half an hour and Hamidou finally accepts the "Baksheesh" in return...

A BURLAP BAG comes flying over the WALL of the COURTYARD late at NIGHT. Then another comes over, lands in the yard. one is around.

BILLY VOICE

(continuous)

Dope and all kinds of shipments get delivered to Aslan, who re- sells it through his runners. People like Ziat. But one night, it backfired...

A THIRD BAG comes over, gets caught on a hooknail and rips right open. HUNDREDS of yellow PILLS spill out.

CUT:

COURTYARD. The SUN is just coming up in the East. PRAYER can be heard in the distance. Thousands of bombers are scattered all over the courtyard.

BILLY VOICE

(continuous)

There were thousands of yellow nembutols. Aslan as usual had the privilege of going into the courtyard before anybody else to pick up his stuff but...

ASLAN arguing vehemently with a GUARD, in his ragged uniform, who won't open the cell of the FIRST FLOOR KOGUS into the courtyard.

BILLY'S VOICE

(continuous)

...it happened to be a new guard that day and he didn't understand the system.

GUARD

No. It's too early.

ASLAN

Open the fucking Gate, you asshole!
Do you know who I am! You want to get in trouble!

GUARD

(angry)

Hey, I your mother! Get back to your bunk.

ASLAN, red in the face, steps back, suddenly pulling out a little REVOLVER. He promptly shoots the GUARD in both legs and stalks back towards his bunk.

CUT:

PRISONERS rushing out into the COURTYARD, scrambling for the windfall of free nembutols.

THE PRISON DIRECTOR, A balding unimpressive looking man in a western suit, is calling up the circular stone STAIRS to the second story Kogus from the first story. With him are several GUARDS, equally reluctant to move forward. Hamidou is absent.

PRISON DIRECTOR
Aslan...be reasonable. Come down and talk.

ASLAN (OFF)
(from second story)
You come up here and talk!

PRISON DIRECTOR
(not moving)
Aslan... if you give up the gun, you can keep the bullets

BILLY'S VOICE
(continuous)
A week later Aslan had a new gun...
A PHOTOGRAPHER, seedy looking, readies a big old fashioned box of a CAMERA. He snaps the shutter on:

BILLY'S VOICE
...I know all this must sound crazy to you, but this place is crazy...

CUT:
ASLAN and a group of FELLOW GANGSTERS, all impeccably dressed and grinning for camera, fresh from their victory.
BILLY, ERICH, MAX, form their own group; in contrast to the Turks, none of them are smiling, MAX has his YOUNG CAT in hand. The PHOTOGRAPHER is lining up his shot, posing them like actors.

BILLY
(continuous)
Everything is "sula-bula" which means "like this, like that" - you never know what will happen. One day one of the new kids was raped in the children's kogus, so they picked out six of the worst kids...
COURTYARD. GUARDS pull out SIX KIDS by the ears from a line-up.

CUT:
CLOSE KID being pinned onto his back on the floor in
CHILDREN'S KOGUS: then he is bent over double by a wooden bench; and TWO GUARDS sit on each end of the bench, holding him down. A silence,
HAMIDOU appears in a hat and mohair suit with narrow lapels, accompanied by his two little fat SONS, also in their Sunday best. With a ceremonious solemnity, HAMIDOU takes off his jacket, hat, vest, hands them to his sons.
BILLY watches through the WINDOW with OTHER PRISONERS.

HAMIDOU is passed a falaka stick. He raises it high in the air and begins to whack at the buttocks, legs, and feet of the SCREAMING KID.

ANOTHER ANGLE - On this cue, the five GUARDS on the other benches begin whacking away; the KIDS squirm, scream, struggle but the GUARDS sitting on the of the benches brace their legs farther apart to keep their balance, In immediate background, the other KIDS watch, scared.

THE TWO SONS with wide-eyed but passive expressions, stare at their father at work.

HAMIDOU beating his VICTIM, screams out:

HAMIDOU
PIS! PIS"
("Obscene, filthy")
Then stops.

BILLY WATCHES AS:
HAMIDOU is handed back his vest, jacket and hat by his
SONS: Puts them on ever so neatly and leads them off as if on a Sunday stroll leaving the CRYING behind. On their backs, we hear, placidly:

HAMIDOU
You see Mamur, Mamet - what happens when you're not a good boy.

BILLY VOICE
(continuos)
Then there's Ziat. The more I know of him...

CUT:
TEN DOLLAR BILL exchanging HANDS. The dirty nails of ZIAT clutch the bill, waving it to the candlelight to see if it is authentic his milky white EYE across the BILL. He is next to his bunk at night.

BILLY VOICE
...the more hate him.
MAX and BILLY are next to him, MAX eagerly gouging with his knife into a small bar of SOAP:
PULLS out a ball of HASHISH inside, neatly concealed. Brings it up to his NOSE, sniffing.
ANOTHER ANGLE - BILLY is watching with glazed eyes - stoned.
Approving of the $10, tucks it into his belly cloth looking over and scowling at:
MAX'S YOUNG CAT on his bunk scratching playfully at one of his wool sweaters.
ANOTHER ANGLE MAX holding the ball of hash:

MAX
Ten dollars for this shit? You greedy one-eyed git.

ZIAT

NO! Is good!
(gets his English wrong)
Me good shit.
(Meaning my shit is good)

MAX
No! You big shit!
ZIAT thinking MAX is correcting his English, nods and repeats:

ZIAT
Yeah! Efe big shit.
BILLY and MAX snigger and ZIAT realizes they are making fun of him. He hates that and suddenly reaches over and:

ZIAT
JAAAASH!
SHAKES THE CAT hard off his bunk. A SQUEAL from the cat.
MAX surprised, glares at Ziat.

MAX
You asshole!
Then hurries after it, calling its name...

MAX
Hikmet come here boy. Hikmet
ZIAT shrugs. So what?

BILLY
(irritated)
What is it with you man, what the hell is it?

ZIAT
Cat, ah! Ayip!

BILLY
You're ayip!

ZIAT
(glares at him, then lets it go)
Look, you don't fuck with me, I don't fuck with you, right?

BILLY
But you fuck with me. You fuck with me all the time. You make crummy tea. You rip us off on the hash.

ZIAT

(amused)
I make special tea for you, Hiyes, okay? We've to live like brothers.
We have to be in here together.

BILLY
(tired of it)
Oh shove it, Ziat for all the money you have, you have nothing!
ZIAT grins, shrugs, squats and fiddles with his keys and footlocker.

ZIAT
You 'Merican. You don't know.
BILLY watches, repulsed and fascinated.

BILLY
Know what?

ZIAT
Was..
(makes gesture with his fingers)
...seven years old. I was on street in Suk. Buy. Sell. No family to take care. I learn.

BILLY
Learn what?
ZIAT shrugs. He thinks BILLY is an idiot.

ZIAT
Dog eat dog, Hi-yes. You fuck other man before he fuck you.
(grins)
And you must fuck last.

BILLY
That's a great philosophy.

ZIAT
(shakes his head)
You 'Merican. You don't know.
MAX has followed his cat down to the end of the floor but it has run up into a rafter which he cannot reach. He calls up.

MAX
Here Hikmet! Come down here boy!
Hikmet...
RAFTER Nothing.
Max gives up.

MAX

Sodding cat!

He shuffles off back to his bunk.

THE CAT is back on ZIAT'S BUNK - NIGHT scratching with his paw around the radio. of the neck, hard. Suddenly he is

GRABBED by the scruff of the neck, hard.

CUT:

BILLY jerks up from his bunk as he the hears a loud, piercing SCREECH, OFF, echoing through the Kogus. Then silence.

CUT:

ZIAT, industrious as always, is preparing his tea on the three burners of the small bottled gas' stove in THE

KITCHEN, FIRST FLOOR Kogus; needless to say the area is filthy with scraps all over the floor, cats and two large wooden eating tables occupied by some PRISONERS. The Kitchen opens up in background into a WASHING ROOM with SINK. It is EARLY MORNING - Muslim CHANTING OFF,

THREE TURKISH PRISONERS walk in, talking (AD LIB), followed by MAX stoned, who shuffles over to the table, about to sit, sees something.

HIS CAT, dead stabbed, and lying there neglected in the corner, just another scrap ready to be swept out.

ZIAT calmly pours the tea for the table, paying MAX no attention, an excellent actor. Prominently seated, however, is a GUARD.

MAX quietly glares at ZIAT and the Guard but says nothing; he has been in prison long enough to know how to hold it in.

ANOTHER ANGLE

MAX - silently walks over and gently picks up the corpse in his arms, starts to walk out.

CUT:

BILLY listening impassively to:

YESIL the lawyer. They are in a booth in the VISITING

CAMBER. Bars separate prisoner and visitor.

YESIL

(smiling)

The new American Ambassador here is following your case very closely.

He says there is progress. But there is another route that is quite possible...

(lowers his voice and leans close)

...For the proper amount of money it is possible I can convince certain officials to lose track of your papers before the High Court in Ankara confirms the sentence of the Lower Court in Istanbul... You would not exist; and you could be in Greece by the time the Turkish courts discovered a stupid clerical mistake...But I have to act before the official sentence is handed down, and for that I must pay certain officials in advance...

BILLY closes his eyes as YESIL'S VOICE drones on, explaining the details, the cast, the simplicity Of it, FADING OUT

UNDER:
BILLY walking the COURTYARD counting his paces 48, 49, 50
Turns, goes back.

SUSAN'S VOICE
...My dearest Billy. I know it is long and it is hard for you, but your family and I are thinking about you all the time. I am trying hard to make enough money nights to come and see you. Your father says that lawyer Yesil wants another
$2000. I know you distrust him more and more, but your father wants to do everything he can, and he is borrowing all he can on the mortgage of the house. Money seems to be the only way out of there.
Except of course the other way...
BILLY, MAX and BELL (bandaged around the ass from the stabbing) are huddled around BELL's BUNK late NIGHT candle burning, a sheet sealing off some of the kogus. Bell furtively looks around, pulling out and elaborately unfolding a set of DRAWINGS from a pack of letters.

SUSAN'S VOICE
(continuous)
...But I cannot say I am for it.
Nor are your parents. They consulted the priest, and he said to send you money for that reason would be like sealing your death.

BELL
(excited)
The blueprints!

MAX
To what?

BELL
The prison, man. There was this
German cat an architect in the hospital. He was helping the Turks build some shit round the place.
I laid some bread on him and he let me copy them.
BILLY, puzzled, turns the drawings upside-down, sideways.
THE DRAWINGS are a lunatic mess of scrambled lines, dots, crosses.

ANOTHER ANGLE
MAX and BILLY, trying to follow the map, look at each other dubiously.

MAX
Too bad you didn't have a machine.

BELL
(intent)
There's two ways out I figger - over the roof, but that's only one person, maybe two. The other way is Under.

BILLY
Tunnel?

BELL
(grins)
It's already built! There's a basement substructure where they used to keep weapons and stuff, but beneath that there's these old catacombs that the Christians built
'bout a thousand fucking years ago to bury their dead. We're sitting right on top of it -- here.
INSERT DRAWING, illustrating roughly the structure of the prison. His FINGER tracing, bubbling with nervous enthusiasm.

BELL (OVER)
The Kraut said there's a whole bunch of hollow sealed shafts sort of like dumbwaiters running along this wall; one of them is right in there, right next to our shower.
We get in there, he says, we can get down into the catacombs. With three of us working....
(stops)
MAX is standing, tapping on the wall, listening, a funny look on is face.

MAX
Gotta be here someplace. Thought
I heard a couple of dead Christians singing down there.

ANOTHER ANGLE
BELL
(irritated)
Stop shitting me, man!

BILLY
(trying to be serious)
But how would you get into the shaft, Jimmy?

MAX
I suppose you knock three times and ask for St. Peter.

BELL
(turning on Max)
Hey! I'm getting this together man and I don't need no fucking
Gastro-head along on this trip!

(a fierce look at
Max then back to
Billy)
We go through the wall.

BILLY
(a resigned look on his face)
We go through the wall?

MAX
(quite sure Bell is out of his skull)
We go through the wall.
BELL between BILLY and MAX walking in the COURTYARD continuing intently:

BELL
...The Kraut was right! I checked it out - there's no reinforced steel in those bath walls.
They're real soft from underground seepage--
BELL reaches the wall, turns around and continues Lowers his voice occasionally as
other PRISONERS intersect them.

BELL
(gesturing profusely)
--the water like "'weeps" through the cement, see. Twenty, thirty years, you can almost
push it over.
All we do is use Gastrohead's screwdriver here and scrape the mortar out. Pull out 2, 3
stones, squeeze through, put 'em back, and get our ass down the shaft, It's a two night
operation, maybe three.

MAX
And what do you do when you in the catacombs?

BELL
The catacoombs? Whaddya want, a door? There's miles of em like a sewer system but
they got to come up someplace in Istanbul.
Max is fed up with it now, no longer joking.

MAX
You gotta be fucking crazy! You got stabbed in the ass once too much, sweetheart,
cause you're gonna end up in Section 13, that's what - not the 'catacombs.

BILLY
Section 13?

MAX
(looking at Bell)
Yeah, for the criminally insane.

(looks at Billy)
I was there once for two weeks and it ain't an illusion. It's awful.
Namidou runs it like a death camp, that's where he spends most of his time...

BILLY
Where is it?

MAX
I don' t know. It's someplace down in there....
(points at the ground)
..deep.. A big door...a wheel....
His eyes go back in time, haunted, vague breaks off.

ANOTHER ANGLE
BELL
(low-keyed)
Hey, you know what's gonna get us out of here? It's not a map, Max.
It's our balls. You know what I mean...
(straight at Max,
Billy, very sincere, his eyes almost watering)
...I gotta get laid man, I don't know 'bout you guys, but if I don't get it on soon, I'm...
I'm not gonna make it.

MAX
(under his breath)
Shit.

BELL
Billy?

BILLY
...The roof sounds better to me than digging through a wall. Ziat's round there all the
time. But the roof....
(looks up)
P.O.V. - THE ROOF, its edges visible over the courtyard.
BILLY shakes his head.

BILLY
The bullet percentage is awful high.
A pause. BILLY looks away from BELL'S stare.

BILLY
If I get caught, Jimmy, I'm facing another months. I'd be back up to
3 years, maybe more...
Looks down.
BELL understands, deeply disappointed.

BELL
Well fuck it! Choose your own death, babe, I'm taking the roof out of here!
Bell leaves:

CUT:
A LONG DUNGEON CORRIDOR at the end of it, the frame of a small; DOOR, cracks
of light at its edges. TRACK IN - F.X. of a siren, capture and now BEATING - heavy
beating from behind that door. CLOSER we reach it. The door FLIES OPEN and
HAMIDOU is glimpsed lighting a cigarette. Like a surreal dream, his hand holding the
match has a thick LEATHER THONG bound around its knuckles and blood speckled
on his fingers.
A BLUR of foreground movement a GUARD coming out the door - dragging:
BELL by the hair across the floor. His face contorting in agony.

BILLY'S VOICE
Dear Susan. Poor Jimmy was caught and beaten so badly he got a severe hernia and lost
a testicle. He's been in the hospital for months having operations..

CUT:
CLOSE BILLY'S TOOTH BEING PULLED
BILLY VOICE
(continuous)
...In comparison my problems seem very small. But two and a half years have now gone
by, and in their own fashion, the Turks are slowly draining my life away...
WIDEN to a STONE CHAMBER and a crazy looking DENTIST in a filthy long white
smock, puffing on a cigarette holder, his ashes falling over Billy as he works his mouth.
A motorized drill is plugged into the wall, adjacent a filthy spittoon covered with blood;
dried blood is spattered liberally around the chamber.
BILLY spits out the blood and looks in the mirror.

BILLY'S VOICE
...I have problems with my stomach and my leg muscles feel very weak.
My gums seem to be shrinking and they sometimes bleed when I massage them...
They've pulled five of my teeth...
Suddenly he starts SHOUTING angrily in TURKISH. The DENTIST screams back at
him. AD LIB.
THE DENTIST still screaming, leans BILLY back in the chair and looks in his mouth.

BILLY'S VOICE
(continuous)
...sometimes they null the wrong one...

CUT:

BILLY is washing himself in his undershorts at the SINK with ERICH; the hot water is on full blast and billows of vapor fill the small stone room, like a sauna. He pours a pitcher full of hot water over his head; his eyes lingering on:
THE STONES of the wall with their cracked moldings; some areas are noticeably darker than others - Bell's "wet spots", the alternate escape route.

BILLY VOICE
(continuos)
...even my dreams don't seem to work any more. Because the outside doesn't seem real any more. It's not even a fantasy...because there is no fantasy.
ERICH uses a coarse washing sponge on BILLY's back.

BILLY'S VOICE
(continuous)
Even masturbation has become boring.
It teaches you, like the rest of prison life, to seal up your emotions, and this is the greatest danger, this is what makes so many of the men change into something monstrous...
EYES of the ARABS peer through the musky vapors at Billy and Erich; they loll about the door curious, lecherous for their bodies.

CUT:
ERICH massaging BILLY on his bunk in the SECOND STORY KOGUS.

BILLY VOICE
(continuous)
It is Erich who has taught me how it is to be conscious, to channel and direct my energy. He has convinced me to stop smoking hashish, he is the calmest man I have ever known. If you don't control your energy in here if can blow you apart like with Bell. And you can't waste it either. You have to weigh up every one of your actions - for and against. Too little sex, too much sex either will throw you off balance...
ERICH leans forward and kisses a tentative BILLY on the lips. A gentle kiss. They are standing inside the TOILET
STALL; lower themselves down onto the seat. ERICH looks back over his shoulder, guarding their privacy. It is late

NIGHT.
BILLY VOICE
(continuously)
...he has taught me about feelings, and the need to express them. And he has taught me about love...
BILLY closes his eyes, softly - and with hesitation - returns ERICH's caress. Their hands probe each other's bodies.

BILLY VOICE
(continuous)

...and what love really is, beyond its physical forms.. .I think up to now I have only considered my own self, never really another...

CUT:
ERICH and BILLY do yoga positions together EARLY MORNING fully clothed, in the FIRST FLOOR KOGUS empty space. ERICH lies on his belly, his back stiffly arched, feet raised.
BILLY stands silent, balanced lightly on his feet, his palms pressed together beneath his chin, centering, eyes closed.

BILLY VOICE
...and now strange as it seems,
Susan, without having seen you in so long I feel myself more inside of you than ever before. I feel your female mind. I sense you, touch you; ...know you; and find myself falling more and more... in love with you.
BILLY rises gracefully onto his toes, stretching his arms out above his head. It is the beginning posture, his body greeting the day.
BILLY and ERICH sit silently now in lotus position, facing each other, breathing slowly, relaxing minds still, looking into each other's eyes. Billy closes eyes.

BILLY
(chant-like, gathering momentum)
A prison a monastery a cloister a cave,
Prison monastery cloister cave,
Prison monastery cloister cave,
Prison monastery cloister cave,
Prison monastery cloister...
SOUND OFF, interrupting the clomp of FOOTSTEPS on the

STAIRS.
ZIAT comes down, staring at the two of them as he goes into the KITCHEN to prepare early morning tea.
BILLY's expression changes.

BILLY
Prison.
Rises from his position.

CUT:
THE SUN flowering up over ISTANBUL.
BILLY rises from his BUNK to the chanting drone of "Allah
Wakbah" OFF, and moving to the closest wall, takes out an old wet rag.

BILLY'S VOICE
Dear Susan. Erich has been transferred to a prison back in

Sweden. He has profoundly affected my life and though I am lonely without him I am calmer than ever...

BILLY erases out a scraped numeral (54) on the wall and with a chalky piece of rock, inscribes in bold strokes the numberal: 53

BILLY'S VOICE
(continuous)
Though I only have 53 days left, I feel I have never been so well adjusted to prison and to living as now....

BELL (OFF)
Allah fuck Off!
JIMMY BELL wakes, hearing the perpetual "Allah Wakbah"

CHANT.
BELL
Asina Covaciml.
(I stick it in his mouth)
He is noticeably pale and weaker than before.

BILLY'S VOICE
(continuous)
...Poor Jimmy...
BILLY cuts hair in the FIRST FLOOR there with a disturbed tight look on his face, work with a pocket mirror. BELL sits inspecting the

BILLY VOICE
(continuous)
...Though his health is bad he still won't give up...
GUARD approaching with a slip in hand.

BILLY'S VOICE
(continuous)
...He still talks of escape.
THE GUARD hands the slip to BILLY who is pleasantly surprised. A visitor.
BILLY, walking down and turning a CORRIDOR into: in the
PRISON, following a GUARD and turning into:
THE VISITING ROOM where the little booths with BARS separate prisoner and visitor. Behind the grill is the Consul,
STANLEY DAVIS. His face is grim and grey. BILLY senses it immediately.

BILLY
What's wrong?

DAVIS
Sit down a moment, Billy. I'm afraid I have some bad news for you.

BILLY sits, tense.

BILLY
Something happen to Dad?... Mom?
DAVIS swallows hard, not to say it

DAVIS
No... It looks like your going to have a new court.

BILLY
What do you mean?

DAVIS
The Prosecutor objected to your sentence for possession; he wanted a smuggling conviction and the
High Court in Ankara reviewed it.

ANOTHER ANGLE
BILLY
And?

DAVIS
We've been notified that they rejected the sentence...
Billy's face drains of all expression.

DAVIS
(continuing)
There were 35 judges on the High
Court. Twenty eight of them voted for a life sentence.
BILLY'S EYES. Numb, dazed, surreal.

DAVIS (OFF)
The Lower Court in Istanbul will have to go along with the decision.
The Judge likes you and he'll do the only thing he can do under the law.... . He'll reduce the sentence to thirty years... We're notified...
Billy.
Suddenly he is GRABBED by his ivy-league striped tie and his face is yanked up to the bars, his glasses falling off.
BILLY is berserk, his face right up against the bars,
GRIPPING Davis tight.

BILLY
What do you mean LIFE FOR FOR WHAT!

FOR WHAT!
DAVIS

(choking)
Billy! Please!
Commotion OFF as GUARDS run in, HAMIDOU in the lead.

BILLY
FOR WHAT! FOR WHAT!
The GUARDS try to pry loose BILLY'S strangling grip ON
DAVIS' tie.

BILLY
I HAVE FIFTY THREE DAYS LEFT!
HAMIDOU takes out a KNIFE and cuts the consul's tie in half. DAVIS falls backwards.
BILLY is hauled now. back, still gripping half the tie.
He is trembling now.

BILLY
I HAVE FIFTY THREE DAYS LEFT!
DAVIS is shaken. He has red bar marks across his face and is absent-mindedly trying
to adjust half a tie as he looks at:
BILLY being hauled out by HAMIDOU, SCREAMING something indistinct.

CUT:
COURTROOM. Same as before.
BILLY, in the prisoner's dock, addresses the Court; as he speaks, a Turkish
TRANSLATOR. drones underneath his voice level:

BILLY
...What is the crime? And what is the punishment? The answer seems to vary from place
to place, and from time to time. What's legal today is suddenly illegal tomorrow cause
some society says it's so; and what's illegal yesterday all of a sudden gets legal today
because everybody's doing it and you can't throw everybody in jail. Well I'm not saying
this is right or wrong.
It's just the way things are....
YESIL the lawyer; DAVIS the consul.
THE PRESS GIRL from the previous trial in the short skirt.

BILLY
BILLY
(continuous)
But I spent the last three and a half years of my life in your prison and I think I paid for
my error and if it's your decision today to sentence me to more years, I...

I...
(a break)
You know my lawyers told me 'be cool

58

Billy don't get upset, don't get angry, if you're good I can maybe get a pardon, an amnesty, an appeal, this that and the other thing.'
Well that's been going down now for 35 years...
YESIL looks over, surprised he is talking like this. Looks at DAVIS.

BILLY.
BILLY
(continuous)
And I've been playing it cool and
I've been good and now I'm damn tired of being good cause you people gave me the belief that I had 53 days left. You hung 53 days in front of my eyes and then you took those 53 days away, and Mister
Prosecutor! I just wish you could...
PROSECUTOR looks over, through his dark green glasses.

BILLY (OVER)
... stand right here where I'm standing and feel what that...
...feels like, cause then you'd know something you don't know you'd know what means, Mister Prosecutor and you'd know the concept of a society is based on the quality of its mercy means, of its sense of fair play, its sense of justice... but
(shrugs and scoffs at himself)
I guess that's just like asking a bear to shit in a toilet...
TRANSLATOR stops, looks puzzled.

BILLY
BILLY
(same self-mocking tone)
For a nation of pigs, it's funny you don't eat them. Fuck it, give me the sentence. Jesus forgave the bastards, but I can't. I hate you.
Nation. I hate your I hate your people. And I fuck your sons and daughters!
Sits down, disgusted; under his breath:

BILLY
...cause you're all pigs.
SILENCE in the uncomfortably. courtroom. PEOPLE looking at each other DAVIS looks down.
YESIL flips some pages abstractedly.

TRANSLATOR SCARED:
TRANSLATOR
Would Your honor like me to translate?
THE OLD CHIEF JUDGE, the same one as before Shakes his head.

JUDGE
That won't be necessary

ANOTHER ANGLE - THE JUDGE turns to BILLY in the foreground rises, and unexpectedly crosses his wrists out in front of him.

JUDGE
(emotionally)
My hands are tied by Ankara!
Makes the gesture of the hands forcefully, with anger.

TRANSLATOR (OFF)
My hands are tied by Ankara!

BILLY WATCHING,
JUDGE (OFF)
I must sentence you, Vilyum Hiyes...

JUDGE
JUDGE
... to be imprisoned at Sagamilcar for a term no less than thirty years...Getchmis olsun

TRANSLATOR (OFF)
"I must sentence you, Vilyum Hiyes, to be imprisoned at Sagamilcar for a term no less than years...
"Getchmis Olsun"
As he translates, the JUDGE unable to control his emotion exits rapidly, not looking at Billy, followed by the TWO

OTHER JUDGES.
TRANSLATOR (OFF)
"May it pass quickly."

CUT:
THREE OLD GLEANING WOMEN swathed in black like three fates turn from their sweeping as BILLY is led out COURTROOM
NUMBER SIX down a long stone corridor. Dust floats through long slanting shafts of yellowish light, like a striped leotard dream. BILLY walks, his eyes straight ahead - determined.

SONG OVER (BELL)
(old Southern blues beat, improvised)
"Mmmmm... got the blues babe,
Got those old Istanbul blues,
Said Yeah, I got the blues babe
Got those old Istanbul blues...
Thirty years in Turkey, babe,
Ain't got nothing left to lose..."

CUT:
BELL sings it, strumming sloppily but with feeling on his guitar. BILLY lies, his back up, on his BUNK nearby.

MAX, stoned, sits at the base of the bunk. It is NIGHT.

The song falters, but MAX now joins in, improvising:

SONG OVER (MAX AND BELL)
"Busted at the border
Two keys in my shoes
Said I was busted at the border with two keys in my shoes
An they gave me thirty years, babe
To learn the old Istanbul blues..."

SEVERAL TURKS are partying it up down at the other end of the SECOND FLOOR KOGUS, playing a "sas" - Turkish type guitar, counterpointed by a little drum; the music is stridently Turkish, and one of the men does a belly-dance in underpants with two lemons masquerading as breasts under his shirt. The LOUD TWANGING of Bell's GUITAR can be heard

OFF, interrupting them. They are annoyed.

BELL leading MAX into the next stanza:

SONG OVER (MAX AND BELL)
"I said Lord now save me
Please save me from this pain"

BILLY, touched - listening, thinking.

SONG OVER (OVER)
"I said Lord come and save me,
Come save me from this pain
Come set me free sweet Jesus..."

TURK (OFF)
Hey knock off that shit music...

TWO TURKS from the party walk up, waving at BELL's guitar, annoyed.

TURK
...We're playing the sas.

BELL
(understanding their
Turkish)
Omina koyden your sas!
(Put your sas in your cunt!)

THE TWO TURKS tense, the mood changing.

BELL gets even angrier, puts the guitar aside, ready to spring.

BELL

...And besides that I fuck Allah and I fuck your Muslim mother too...
They don't understand but one of them is reaching into his pants for his shiv.

BELL
You got that, shit face? Asina...

BILLY (OFF)
KNOCK IT OFF!
ANOTHER ANGLE BILLY is moving fast between the TWO TURKS and BELL. A new authority in his voice, and controlled anger in his face.

BILLY
(to Bell)
Cut it! No more fights.
BELL looks.

BILLY
We're getting out of here.
BELL astonished.

CUT:
BILLY, with Max's little screwdriver and a metal spoon, digs hard at the cracks around a dark stone in the SINK
ROOM, FIRST FLOOR KOGUS. With him is MAX working on the same stone. They are sweating, shirtless, looking back over their shoulders at:
BELL guarding the STAIRS.
BILLY works the stucco out, jiggling with the stone (about a nine inch circumference) using his fingers and screwdriver. Painful work.

BILLY'S VOICE
Dear Susan. It's taken me a long time to find out that it's got to stop somewhere. I've learned painfully not to trust the Turks, the courts, the lawyers, the Consul, the United States Government, and not even my loving parents. There is only one way out of here.. The
Midnight Express.
BILLY kicks with his sneakers at the stone, as silently as possible. A LOUD NOISE - crumbling dust, stucco.
BELL at the stairs freezes, fearful. Then SILENCE. He
Runs over.

MAX, BELL, BILLY.
MAX
(in a whisper)
We're undermining the other stones!
BELL studies it, pointing to the stone above left the one that has been loosened.

BELL
We gotta take a chance and do that one next -
(pointing)
Then pull out this one -
(pointing to the one directly left of the loosened stone, excited)
Just jiggle it, scratch it out, loose nit up, it's soft real soft!
BILLY has his head pressed close to the loosened stone.
Suddenly:

BILLY
It's there!

BELL
What?

BILLY
Listen!
ANOTHER ANGLE - all THREE press their ears to the stone.
A silence. The faintest whisper of WIND and dripping 'WATER - indicating a shaft of
some nature. BELL looks back at BILLY.

BELL
I told you, I told you you cock- suckers! You didn't believe me.
BILLY smiles. MAX reaches over and grabs Bell's face between his hands, kisses him
violently.

MAX
Fuck me! You beautiful mother, you!

CUT:
MAX now on guard at the STAIRS, looks over at:
BELL AND BILLY - with fresh paste putting the finishing touches on the edges of the
stone which has been replaced in its original position. Bell's half naked torso reveals a
pair of dice with lucky sevens tattooed on his shoulder.

CUT:
THE REPLACED STONE. On close inspection, it is apparent that the stucco around it
doesn't match the other stones one bit, but as we PULL BACK to see ZIAT washing his
tea cups in the SINK during the DAY, this irregularity is lost in the greater mosaic of
the wall structure. At least ZIAT doesn't notice as:
BILLY nervously comes into the SINK area, watching him, and calls to him.

BILLY
(using Turkish)
Hey, Ziat, hurry up with the tea will ay!

ZIAT
(mutters to himself)
Work, work, work, that's all do

BILLY
I don't hear you bitch about the money.
BILLY followed by ZIAT into the KITCHEN casts a look of relief at:
BELL and MAX who wait at a table with empty tea cups.

CUT:
A HORDE OF COCKROACHES stream out from a crack in the stone as BILLY and MAX dig, scrape, jiggle the third stone. Both covered with sweat, working with confidence now.
A DARK EMPTY SHAFT on the other side. Dripping water. Two stones removed.
BELL runs over:

BELL
Want me to take over?

BILLY
You want to split your hernia again?

MAX
Get off our tits!
Bell turns to go. Suddenly a LOUD CRUMBLING NOISE and:
A FOURTH STONE starts to go - but brakes itself.
BILLY, MAX, BELL all framed in a posture of fear -- not daring to move.
SECOND STORY KOGUS remains silent.
BELL looks up the STAIRS, tiptoes back, indicating they are clear.
MAX AND BILLY. All THREE of them look:
THE THREE A HALF STONE SPACE. Easily big enough for them to squeeze through.
BILLY shines a candle in the shaft,

OFF.
THE THREE look at each other. The same thought. Eager eyes.
The TRAIN WHISTLES by in the night, OFF.

BELL
(sudden)
Let's go!
BILLY looks at his watch, hates to do it. Shakes his head.

BILLY
No. No time. Put 'em back.
MAX groans to himself.

CUT:

BILLY tense and restless at his BUNK TWILIGHT. A loud RADIO
OFF - Turkish News.

BILLY

We go early. Any fuck-ups we should be back here and have the stones in by dawn.
ANOTHER ANGLE - MAX, BELL, AND BILLY. A pause.

BILLY

You got your stuff?

MAX

Yeah.

BELL

(persistent)
Haps, railroad, bus timetables?

MAX

(business-like)
Everything.

BILLY

Okay.
(looks around the group)
Let's do it.
He extends his hands and the other two cross in a six-handed shake.

CUT:

MAX signals down the STAIRS - "all clear".
BILLY going through the HOLE in the STONES that NIGHT into:
A DARK SHAFT spookily leading downwards. He lights a thick
CANDLE tied horizontally across his sneakers so as to give him his light source where
his footholds are. His P.V.O:
PART DUMBWAITER SHAFT, PART WATER WELL from a previous century A
series of corrugated mossy old footholds and iron spikes lead down at irregular
intervals.

CUT:

BILLY, MAX AND BELL, each with their own foot candle, are spaced along the shaft
easing downwards. BILLY looks up at
MAX about ten feet above.

BILLY

Okay?

MAX
Yeah!

BILLY
Jimmy?

BELL
(struggling.)
What?

BILLY
How's your hernia?

BELL
Don't make me laugh.
BILLY in a sweat, slips. A tense moment - then he catches himself. OFF - the TRAIN WHISTLE can be heard, echoing into the shaft.Mixed suddenly with LOUD TALKING OFF. Arguing in Turkish. BILLY freezes, signals upwards with a sharp hiss of breath.

VOICE #1 (OFF)
What do you mean, you forgot, he'll have my ass!

VOICE #2 (OFF)
Well I can't do two things at once, you were supposed to be here at nine o'clock!
BILLY identifying the relative location of the voices, eases downwards, coming to a GRILL, looks in at:
A BASEMENT ROOM with FURNACE. TWO TURKISH GUARDS throw the prison rubbish in the furnace, still arguing, AD LIB.
BILLY signals upwards.
REVERSE ANGLE, from inside the basement, of BILLY slipping past the grill, his face sharply illuminated by the flame of the furnace.
Off the walls around the grill we can see the GIANT
SILHOUETTES of the two guards still arguing.
BILLY comes to the base of the shaft. A puddle of scummy water. Unstraps the candle. A current of WIND He peers around.

P.O.V. - A WINDING NARROW CATACOMB, WITH BEEHIVE BURIAL PLACES ON BOTH SIDES.
BILLY, sniffing the stench, unrolls a ball of THREAD ties it to a marker and heads in.

CUT:
BILLY, BELL and MAX are in the catacomb. A scratchy hideous sound and:
BATS fly out squealing from the ceiling.
THE BOYS hit the ground as BATWINGS flap over them, colliding against each other, knocking off walls,
SCREECHING, then diminishing in sound. Fewer and fewer.

Then gone.

MAX
(looking up, scared)
Jesus!
BILLY looking up.

BILLY
Anybody bitten?

ANOTHER ANGLE
BELL
Nah, just covered with batshit!

BILLY
(getting to his knees)
They went out over there: must be some kind of exit.
Heads in that direction.

CUT:
A HUGE SPIDER scatters off, as BILLY's CANDLE illuminates:
ANOTHER ENDLESS WALKWAY. BILLY comes to a stop - frustrated.

BILLY
Let's go back the other way.
INTERSECTION Two walkways. BELL leads in, unwinding the thread, stops.

BELL
(desperate)
The fuck are we?
BILLY comes into view, equally frustrated.

BILLY
What time is it?

MAX
Two thirty.
ANOTHER MAZE of walkways. The three stop exhausted, faces blackened. BILLY,
in utter rage and frustration starts kicking the wall.

BILLY
Shit! Shit! Shit!

MAX
(slumping to the ground)
It's a dead end. The Turks musta' sealed it up.

BELL
What the fuck we gonna do?
SILENCE as the three pathetic escapees ponder their fate.
BILLY, getting a grip on himself, thinking.

BILLY
We go back.

ANOTHER ANGLE
MAX
What? You gotta be joking.

BILLY
(resolute)
We go back, seal it up again, and come in tomorrow night - every night 'till we get out
of here.
There's gotta be a way. Those bats got out someplace.
(rises)
Now let's go. Doubletime!
Takes the THREAD and starts to follow it back.

CUT:
THE SHAFT. BILLY leads the climbers UP.
MAX reaches a new foothold, stops, getting his breath.
Looks down at BELL heavy breathing OFF. Urging him on.

MAX
You gotta have a lot of balls for this
BELL, suffering, can't help but grin.

BELL
(murmurs)
Count me out.
(to himself, shaking his head)
Who ever heard of anybody sneaking back into a fucking jail?
MAX overhearing it.

MAX
Yeah, what if got caught?
BELL starts to giggle.

BILLY (OFF)
(up the shaft)
Hey Max, don't make the dummy laugh.
MAX laughing, shaking his head.

MAX
(between giggles)
Who's laughing? I mean I find this terribly depressing... Can you see old Hamidou's face when he tries to figure this one out?
BILLY can't go on, starts to giggle at the thought.

BILLY
(between giggles)
We'll tell him we were checking out our escape route. We wanted to be completely sure before we tried it.
ANOTHER ANGLE - the THREE of them, spaced along the shaft, are all giggling hysterically. Echoing. HOLD ON them.

CUT:
BILLY comes through the HOLE in the stones in the SINK
AREA. It is still NIGHT. He looks around - silence. MAX follows through the hole.

CUT:
BILLY and MAX work fractically to seal up the STONES.
BELL, exhausted, is at the STAIRS guarding. Distant early morning SOUNDS of prison waking up. We feel they will be spotted this time, but:

CUT:
BILLY slumps into his BUNK as the first rays of LIGHT come up in the sky and the CHANT from the Mosque commences. He immediately sinks into sleep.
CLOSE on OLD TEA LEAVES being washed in the SINK. A MILKY
WHITE EYE follows into view. ZIAT is preparing his early morning tea, his good eye now moving to something beyond the tea leaves. Curious, he straightens, throwing the withered bunch of leaves the sink.
ZIAT approaches the irregular stucco paste around the
REPLACED STONES; runs his fingers along the ridges, noticing the paste is fresh.
BILLY snoring from fatigue. BELL wakes him quickly.

BELL
Billy, wake up! They found it!
OFF there is a lot of SHOUTING downstairs.

BILLY
Who?

BELL
Ziat!

CUT:
BILLY standing in a group of PRISONERS with BELL and MAX.

69

He has a look of total despair on his face, as he watches.
THE SINK. PRISONERS are everywhere jabbering excitedly among themselves. ZIAT is conferring with HAMIDOU as GUARDS rip out the last stone, revealing the HOLE leading to the

SHAFT.
BILLY's gaze shifts to ZIAT fixing all his hatred on him.
ZIAT grinning, moves away, and his falaka stick cocked like a sergeant major - moves among the prisoners.

HAMIDOU
Shut up!
They all fall immediately silent. HAMIDOU continues his walk among them, bypassing:
MAX who shifts his gaze onto:
BILLY. HAMIDOU approaches, his eyes moving over BILLY with contempt, and shifting him aside with the stick. To him Billy is the same passive prisoner as before. He moves on, shifting OTHERS aside and then stops at:
BELL. HAMIDOU swings his stick up slowly and taps him lightly on the chest. BELL realizes and is afraid.

HAMIDOU
No do! No do! I tell you I see you again.. Finish!
He punctuates this last with a theatrical tap on the chest and he gestures to the GUARDS.

HAMIDOU
Take him!
BELL, already broken by bad beatings, shivers.

BELL.
No! Oh no! No...
GUARDS grab him, hurry him out the Kogus behind HAMIDOU
BILLY holds himself rigid, trying not to break. Bell's
PROTESTS continue OFF.
MAX unable to contain his anger, strides right up to ZIAT, collars him, livid.

MAX
You bastard! This time I'm gonna kick your fucking brains all over this kitchen!

ZIAT
(calm)
Fine. Good. Man to man. We fight now. And when finish I bring
Hamidou and he kick you fuckinq ass.
MAX is about to swing when BILLY grabs him.

70

BILLY
Max! Cool it!
(looking at Ziat calmly)
Ziat's just doing his job.
ZIAT Glances from BILLY back to MAX fixing on him as BILLY walks him away.

CUT:
MAX is at his BUNK that NIGHT; puts away the hypodermic needle, stoned and speeding at the same time, smoking a cigarette. BILLY inwardly tense, sits with his head in his hands.

MAX
Bell's gonna talk. They got to find out. Man, we gotta out.
Tears have formed in his eyes.

MAX
Goddamn Gastro's killing me. Making me blind. Hey Billy!

BILLY
(sympathetic)
Yeah.

MAX
I got some acid man. Maybe we can drop some on the guards huh? In their tea or something.
BILLY looks away, not even considering. But MAX is caught up in the notion.

MAX
Yeah I got it all worked out.
Billy, listen to me.
(looks at Billy, his eyes glazed)
That old guard likes you, You drop some acid on him. When he's Seeing rainbows yer know. walk out - tonight.

BILLY
Then we're outside the kogus.
Then what?

MAX
What?

BILLY
After we're outside the kogus?

MAX
Oh we... we...

BILLY
Max... Your BILLY shirt's on fire...
MAX clumsily brushes the burning ash off his shirt where it's made a hole.

MAX
Oh shit! Oh Christ!
His eyes cloud with tears. He sits down, head between his hands.

MAX
There just comes a time you know... you know you're never going to git it on.
Suddenly shifts mood again, stands, pulling out a SHIV, resolute, eyes brightening.

MAX
That's what I'm gonna do.
(giggles)
BILLY looks up wondering.

BILLY
What?

MAX
(crazily)
Cut his fucking throat.

BILLY
Whose?

MAX
ZIAT... What do I got to lose huh!
What do I got to lose. And I'd really enjoy it.
Lurches against the bunk.

BILLY
Max, sit down. You're in no shape to kill anybody.

MAX
I want to cut his throat.

BILLY
It's already been cut.

MAX
Then I'll cut his balls off.
BILLY smiles, shakes his head, then:

BILLY
If you really wanted to hurt Ziat
(pause)
MAX slumps back down on the bunk, suddenly tired of killing.

BILLY
(reflective)
...His money - steal that, you steal his blood... Could you see his face when everything he worked so hard to get got snatched?
(plays with the thought idly, then shrugs)
If we knew where he hid it.
(waves it away)
Anyway, steal from him they'd pick up the whole prison and shake it sideways. We couldn't hide it anywhere.

MAX
(head bobbing now, murmurs)
You know where it is?

BILLY
What?

MAX
(a vague grin)
I know where it is.
BILLY glances at him, not sure whether he heard.

BILLY
His money?
MAX gives him a goofy nod - and a grin. Imitating Robert Newton as Long John Silver.

MAX
'Dem dat hides can finds says I'...
I seen him, the clever tit, sneaking looks at it late at night, talking to it.

BILLY
(beginning to believe him)
Yeah? Where?
MAX, distracted, let's his attention wander back. Inaudible his head bobbing now.

MAX
Hishradyo.

BILLY
Max - where?

MAX
(his mouth hanging open, eyes closed)
His radio Back of his open, radio...
He lurches over gently on the bunk.

MAX
That's why he never plays it...
MAX Sleeps.
BILLY surprised, then reflective.

CUT:
THE BACK OF THE RADIO is unscrewed; the cover pulled off.

EMPTY!
MOVE TO ZIAT. The look is as Billy expected. Horror, shock, anger, fear. ZIAT
SCREAMS hysterically like old Greek widow and:
BEATING HIS CHEST and tearing at his hair, ZIAT runs out of the KOGUS wailing,
moaning.

CUT:
THE SECOND STORY KOGUS is being" controlled" by the GUARDS.
WIDE ANGLE reveals a circus of clockwork destruction as the GUARDS, making
abundant NOISE, systematically rip up each bunk, locker, mattress, picture, book, etc.,
their faces flushed with this opportunity for orgy.

CUT:
THE PRISONERS are lined up in the COURTYARD, each one being body
searched.Prominent are MAX and BILLY, looking up amused at the
SECOND STORY WINDOWS - feathers from a mattress fly around.
ZIAT Briefly appears, his face at the window, looking at the prisoners in the yard,
frustrated.
HAMIDOU breaks apart a with his bare hands.
ZIAT is stripping MAX's possessions, sure he will find it here.

VOICE (OFF)
Down here!
Ziat springs up.
GUARD calling out from the STAIRS.

GUARD
We found it!

CUT:

ZIAT leaning in CLOSE, OVER THE STOVE in the KITCHEN, framed by GUARDS. It is the same crouched posture he always uses to work the stove but now his eyes show complete despair as he sees:
A THOUSAND SHREDS OF PAPER MONEY floating in his pots amid his withered tea bags. From ashes to ashes and dust to dust.
ZIAT folds his head into his hands, sobbing then wailing very human, very sad.

CUT:
KITCHEN - NEGDIR an Arab, is now running the tea concession.
A jolly ebullient man. Pours a cup for MAX. Several OTHERS are at the table.

NEGDIR
(heavily accented
English)
...He sell me tea business - everything. No the same. Ziat lose all...
(makes the gesture towards the heart and the gut, using the Arabic word)
Heart! Soul!

MAX
He never had one.

NEGDIR
Soon he go back streets Istanbul.
Thousand enemy. No money.
(makes throat cutting gesture)

MAX
I'll drink to that.
(toasting with the tea)
Just as:
ZIAT enters the kitchen; he eyes Max with hatred, sits at the other TABLE and orders tea. Surprisingly, he is wearing a suit and clean shirt-unlike his usual grimy appearance.
BILLY, looking shaken, enters the kitchen, glances at ZIAT sits with MAX.

BILLY
Just got some news on Bell.

MAX
What?

BILLY
Bad. Sent to the City Hospital.
They ruptured his hernia again.

MAX
(grim)

Oh shit.

BILLY
I Guess he didn't talk...Poor bastard.
BILLY glances over at:
ZIAT drinking tea.

BILLY AND MAX
BILLY
Why the suit?

MAX
Maybe he's changing jobs.

VOICE (OFF)
SAYIM! SAYIM!
BILLY looks over to see:
HAMIDOU and a DOZEN GUARDS spreading through the KOGUS, assembling everybody with shouts of "SAYIM!"

CUT:
THE PRISONERS are lined up in ranks in the FIRST FLOOR

KOGUS.
BILLY glancing at MAX next to him, wondering why.
HAMIDOU goes down the line, his FLUNKIES searching each man.
A GUARD reaches into ZIAT'S pocket and comes out with a matchbox. Yells to HAMIDOU who comes over.

HAMIDOU
(opening the matchbox)
Nebu?
MATCHBOX Containing a small amount of HASHISH.
HAMIDOU reaches over and pulls ZIAT out of the 'line roughly.

HAMIDOU
Nebu?
Starts to slap him around.
BILLY glancing at MAX.

MAX
(worried)
What's going on? Maybe Ziat can't pay off; Hamidou's taking it out in trade.
HAMIDOU smashes ZIAT again, but pulls the punch.

HAMIDOU

Where did you get this hash?
Raises his arm again.

ZIAT
(cowering, pretending fear)
From Max.
Point at:
MAX who stiffens, eyes like cracked eggs.

MAX
(under his breath)
You got to be kidding.
HAMIDOU peers at MAX, advances.

HAMIDOU
What's happening with this hash?
Indicates the matchbox in his hand.

MAX
I didn't sell it to him. I don't have anything to do with this,

I...
HAMIDOU
(leans closer)
I know your face. Where did you get the hash?

BILLY
(interrupting in
Turkish))
(He knows nothing about it. Ziat's lying.

HAMIDOU
(turns on Billy, in
English)
You, goddamn you, shut up!
(Back to MAX)
Take him to the cellar)
GUARDS drag off.

MAX
Get out of here! He's lying! That cock-sucker! Billy...?

CUT:
BILLY sits on his his anger building, his imagination running wild.

CUT:

MAX being dragged down a CORRIDOR by his feet. A SCREAM.

BILLY
CUT:
BELL, his features distorted, being carried into an

AMBULANCE.
CUT:
BELL, MAX and BILLY at the wall, digging together, MAX hugging BELL the time they found the shaft.

CUT:
MAX twisting out of the grip of a GUARD and, grabbing the glass from his smashed spectacles, he cuts deep into his wrist. GUARDS grab him. A LOUD LAUGH OFF carrying over.
BILLY turning on his bunk to see:
ZIAT joking with TWO GUARDS as he enters the SECOND STORY.
The guards back down the stairs.
BILLY already in movement.
ZIAT, in his suit, collecting suitcase from his bunk, preparing to leave.

VOICE (OFF)
ZIAT!
Turns and catches a FIST in the side of the face. Staggers into a bunk.
BILLY, fists clenched, yells a string of Turkish curse words at him:

BILLY
Asina covacim, ipnave pesankek...yosakt.
Lunges.
ZIAT is bulky, throws the smaller BILLY off and scrambles past a bunk.
BILLY is up and after him. Jumps back as a SHIV cuts the air in front of him. His side is cut.
ZIAT holding the shiv, feints, cursing BILLY in Turkish.
BILLY skips back, takes a MATTRESS off the bed and runs it right into KNOCKING HIM AND THE WHOLE BUNK OVER.
THE TWO scramble around, BILLY tackling him into another
BUNK which also goes over. Chairs break.
ZIAT butts his head into BILLY'S jaw.
BILLY staggers back from the blow and ZIAT jumps him, BITING into his ear.
ZIAT, getting a better hold, now BITES into BILLY'S NOSE.
BILLY slams ZIAT in the nose hard with the palm of his hand. ZIAT relinquishes his hold, grabbing at his broken bleeding nose.
BILLY beats him around the head but though the blood now flows and teeth are broken, is like a clumsy bear, hard to kill.
ZIAT scrambles away on his knees under another BUNK now screaming as loud as he can.

ZIAT
HELP ME! GUARDS! HELP ME!
SEVERAL PRISONERS watching from further down the SECOND
STORY Kogus now move in sync, turning on their RADIOS loud as possible, drowning out the cries for help, others watching the stairs.
BILLY takes the BUNK and throws it over, revealing ZIAT cowering in pure terror. He grabs ZIAT by the hair, hauls him up and
LAUNCHES HIS KNEE into HIS FACE.
ZIAT thuds onto the floor.
BILLY stomps him in the gut hard.
ZIAT screams unnaturally shrill.
BILLY, driven by supernatural anger, now jumps on him and
CLAMPS HIS MOUTH right on ZIAT'S open SCREAM.
A STRUGGLING KISS ensues.
BILLY pulls back, his mouth filled with blood, spitting out.
AN UNIDENTIFIED PIECE OF FLESH which Bits the ground with an odd slow motion grace.
ZIAT - CLOSE in terror; throat cords rippling; eyes bulging with disbelief, body quivering, mouth open and screaming, but it is a SILENT SCREAM and the mouth is a dark hole filled with blood and without a TONGUE.
BILLY, without a moment's mercy, crashes his fist into
ZIAT'S face.
ZIAT his strength now broken, collapses on his back.
BILLY crashes his fist again into the hated face. He is
GRABBED now by a GUARD, but:
ANOTHER ANGLE - BILLY shakes the GUARD OFF, then as ANOTHER
GUARD runs up, BILLY SLAMS him aside and, obsessed, lunges back down on ZIAT and
BOTH HANDS CLAMPED TOGETHER high in the air delivers a final blow to ZIAT'S face. The bones shatter. Pause. His ogre unconscious beneath him, BILLY, now in SLOW MOTION,
EXTENDS HIS ARMS IN THE AIR - in the fighter's victory gesture, and his eyes glow with the fever in them, and with his mouth and face bloodied, he looks like a savage.
No longer Billy Hayes.

SHARP CUT:
BILLY bound in a thick leather belt (a kiyis) which screws tightly around the waist and cinches the hands together, is being HAULED in continuing SLOW MOTION through a huge
DOOR somewhere in one of the cavernous corridors of the prison.The door is approximately NINE FEET by SIX FEET, strong and wooden with a circular iron handle which one of the GUARDS now pulls open; a GLIMPSE of darkness within.

THE DOOR CLOSES. SUPERIMPOSE:
SECTION 13 - ASYLUM FOR THE CRIMINALLY INSANE

A YEAR LATER

MAX, barely recognizable in a torn sheet and with a blackened face, comes rushing into a crowded ROOM, screaming louder than any other inmate. marks on his face, He is enraged, blood dripping from scratch ATTENDANTS in white smocks chase him over the beds. Max is yelling in Turkish.

MAX

Please, will you listen to me?
Will someone please listen to me?
JUST LISTEN To ME!

ATTENDANTS

Hamidou! Get Hamidou! Get the
Kiyisl!
The ATTENDANTS wrestle with him, but he throws them off, tearing around the room mindlessly. In the process we see that not much attention is paid him because everybody else is crazy! There are 50 other LUNATICS yelling at each other in fights over sheets, blankets, beds, cigarettes, jumping: screaming, pushing, shoving; some babbling to themselves, rocking, crying, chanting, singing. Several of them (the craziest) are stark naked. some, wrapped in torn blackened sheets, patrol the room like quick ferrets, sharp eyes open for anything they can steal. Others move in meaningless, blank-eyed silence. The walls are filthy black and join the ceilings in arches rather than angles, giving the look of an old dungeon. Fifty beds are lined up right next to each other so that you walk right into your bed. A constant nerve-racking NOISE.
HAMIDOU bursts into the ROOM, the angry look in his eyes spelling real trouble for Max. MOVE with him as he sweep sin on MAX and picks him up with one move and SMASHES HIM against the wall. Max hardly notices.
ANOTHER ANGLE - HAMIDOU takes the leather kiyis from an
ATTENDANT, moves in on MAX and starts clamping it around him.
AN ATTENDANT walks through the room with an apron containing several large pockets bulging with red, green, blue, white
PILLS, which he distributes by the handful.

ATTENDANT

(crying out)
Hop! Hop! Hop! Full moon. Hop!
Hop! Hop!
THE LUNATICS gobble them up as if they were candy. In some of the clustered areas, nine lunatics occupy as little as three beds.
MAX is tightly bound now by HAMIDOU, but his body arches against the bindings, his neck straining, his teeth snapping at the air. HAMIDOU grabs him with one hand by the leather waist, hauls him high up in the air and
THROWS MAX half-ways across the room, MAX smashing heavily against some beds, continuing to SCREAM OFF as:
THE ATTENDANT with the pills-now bypasses BILLY on one of the beds.

ATTENDANT
Hop! Hop! Full Moon - take your pills!
BILLY gobbles them up. He has changed. Lines in his face.
No smile, no sense of humor; a brooding silence about him, a straight ahead look. He pays no attention to MAX off; he is in grubby white pyjamas and shower sandals. Rolls back onto hi& bed with its filthy torn sheet, totally ignoring the surrounding commotion, and
ANOTHER ANGLE - turning onto his shoulder, BILLY suddenly finds himself face to face with a dark saddened visage.
The MAN is very young and stark naked but for an old black rag wrapped around his head and clutched under his chin.
His eyes are yellow, the voice pleading.

YOUNG MAN
Cigare?
(pause, same tone, holds out his palm)
Cigare? Cigare?
BILLY shakes his head sharply --too sharply --and barks, irritable.

BILLY
Go away!
Turns on his other shoulder, trying to sleep.

YOUNG MAN (OFF)
Cigare? Cigare?
YOUNG MAN in a surprisingly meek tone.

YOUNG MAN
S'il Vous plait, Monsieur? S'il vous plait?
BILLY, really aggravated now, springs up from the bed, and in the quirky way the mad and the eccentric adopt walks determinedly away from the young man, looking back to shake his head bizarrely at him one more time.

ANOTHER ANGLE
BILLY walking down the aisle bypasses MAX int he kiyis, rolling on the floor, still screaming in Turkish.

MAX
Will you listen to me? PLEASE LISTEN

TO ME!
Several LUNATICS are gathered around tormenting him, one of them yanking on his penis as if it were made of rubber; another is playing with his ass. A third one, also in a leather kiyis, is leaning over MAX jabbering and drooling into his face.
MAX, more enraged by this than the other bodily offences, lunges up sharply and bites the man's FACE. SCREAMS, etc.

81

BILLY, paying no attention except for a brief disinterested glance, keeps going into:
A SECOND ROOM. MORE LUNATICS. A screaming OLD MAN is chasing after another OLD MAN who has stolen his tespe beads, waving them back at the first old man who howls with rage, frantic to have his beads back. The second old man throws the beads to a THIRD OLD MAN who hops across the beds with the FIRST OLD MAN chasing him. BILLY intersects.

OLD MAN
(pleading)
Allah! Allah! Yok! Yok! Yok!
Brack!
A LITTLE NERVOUS MAN stares into a broken pocket mirror fingering the large round carbuncle under his eye, trying to rub it away with little grimaces and flurries of nervous motion.
TWO ATTENDANTS in smocks indifferently finish eating on a newspaper spread across one of the beds; they shake out the paper.
CHICKEN BONES, ORANGE PEELS hitting the floor. A flurry of movement, as the LUNATICS scuffle like rats over the left- overs. AD LIB curses, yells.
AN OLD MAN obscenely gestures to BILLY from his bed.

OLD MAN
Hey American. Fik! Fick! Come.
Fik! Fik!
His blackened teeth leer.
BILLY, seemingly immune to all of this in some private island of his own madness, walks in his determined way past a PARTITION to:
A CIRCULAR STONE STAIRCASE leading downwards, the stones damp, dark, slippery. BILLY continues with the same straight- ahead determination to:
A LONER LEVEL. at last BILLY's expression changes to almost childish relief, for here at last is the refuge he seeks the relative comfort and silence of THE WHEEL.
It is a grim, squat PILLAR dominating the room and bearing the weight of the ceiling. And around it some SIXTY LUNATICS trudge slowly, near silently, in counter-clockwise flow.
It is a hypnotic shuffle and BILLY blends right in, sliding easily into the sluggish, mindless river, his eyes hanging loosely on the floor, watching:
THE SOOTHING RHYTHM OF FEET shuffling at a comforting pace.
These are the spokes of the wheel.

CUT:
TWO TINY BARE LIGHT-BULBS give faint, eerie illumination to the chamber. One one side, a pot-bellied stove flickers, etching the shadows of the walkers in a strange orange glow.
SOME LUNATICS, not walking, hover around the stove. OTHERS are jammed onto a low L-shaped wooden platform that runs the length of two walls. of these men are naked, covered with open running sores over their knees, elbows, buttocks.

But they are much quieter than the upstairs crowd. They are the lowest order of madmen. They have no minds left.

They are the damned.

BILLY walks among them, expressionless. A tall, thin cadaverous TURK with a grizzled beard now shuffles up alongside BILLY, looks at him, walks with him. is about fifty, his pyjamas relatively clean, looking more sane than the average but his eyes are bright and scary and his wet hair is matted down on his head, and big clumps of it have been pulled out. He speaks with a cultured English accent.

AHMET

You're an American?

BILLY is interrupted but keeps his eyes on the ground.

AHMET doesn't wait for an answer.

AHMET

Ah yes, America! My name is Ahmet.

I studied philosophy at Harvard for many many years. But actually

Oxford is my real Alma Mata -

I've also studied in Vienna. Now I study here.

BILLY doesn't notice, shuffles along.

AHMET

...They put me here. They say I raped a little boy. I have been here very long time. They will never let me go.

BILLY pays no attention, keeps shuffling on. Glances at him, smiles.

AHMET

They won't let YOU go either.

The smug certainty of his manner reaches some chord deep inside Billy, because Billy glances briefly at this lunatic who is smiling. Billy looks back at his feet.

AHMET

No, they'll never let you go.

They tell you they let you go but you stay. You never go from here.

BILLY plods on. grins and tries to explain the situation like a father lecturing a child.

AHMET

You see we all come from a factory.

Sometimes the factory makes bad machines that don't work. They put them here. The bad machines don't know they're bad machines, but the people at the factory know. They know one of the machines that doesn't work...

They walk on. Ahmet's expression changes.

AHMET

(polite)

I think we have spoken enough for today. I say good night to you.

He wraps his rags around himself quite carefully and we
FOLLOW him out of the circle. He drops to his hands and knees and with a sense of dignity, crawls into the filthy blackness under the L-shaped wooden platform, disappearing like a cockroach.
BILLY plods on.

CUT:

AN OLD WHITE-BEARDED MADMAN the Hoja, grandiose in his rags, leads MUSLIM PRAYER in the first ROOM. Some of his followers have prayer mats, others a scrap of sheet or newspaper; their tones discordant, still pushing and shoving at each other during the prayer.
TWO SPASTICS can't follow the routine of kneeling and bending; they tangle up absurdly and fall to the floor in a ball of arms and legs.
A FALAKA STICK pokes BILLY wake SOUND of the CHANTING fills room. It is evidently impossible to distinguish night from day because there are no windows.
ATTENDANTS poke the LUNATICS awake with their "clubs.

ATTENDANTS
Head count! Head count!

CUT:

A MASS OF LUNATICS in the ROOM all at once. Attendants take a redundant and comic head count. The place sounds like a "yadi yadi room" the noise fearsome.

ANOTHER ANGLE
ATTENDANT #1
Sixty two, sixty three, sixty four....

ATTENDANT #2
Seventy four, seventy five, seventy six.. .get back there, you! . . . seventy five, seventy six....)
ATTENDANTS poke around underneath a bed and pull out a very old trembling VEGETABLE.
OTHER ATTENDANTS wrap an old DEAD LUNATIC with no teeth and foam on his open lips into a dirty sheet and haul him away.
BILLY amid the LUNATICS. We MOVE closer and closer to him, the head COUNT regressing. The room has become a torture cell - the NOISE LOUDER, LOUDER, closing in on
Billy.

CUT:
BILLY is led down a CORRIDOR by HAMIDOU into:
A VISITING room - Cabins are lined up like narrow wooden phone booths.

HAMIDOU
Kabin on-yedi

BILLY plods without interest to the specified cabin, closes the door, sits in the chair. No one is there. He waits - indifferent to any sense of time. Dirty two glass panes separate visitor and prisoner booths; bars are between the panes. An erratic microphone is the method of communication, giving a weird and distant aspect to the voice.

HAMIDOU opens a small peep-hole in the cabin door, looks in unseen as:

TEE VISITOR DOOR opens and SUSAN tentatively walks in holding a large photo album; it takes several moments for her to react, and then her face shows the shock.

BILLY stares at her, his face rabid, decaying; if he remembers her even, he doesn't register it because she is a shock to him as well. Reality, the outside world all at once. His mind is spinning, unbalanced, unable to grasp it.

SUSAN (OFF)
Oh my God...!

SUSAN
SUSAN
Billy, what have they done to you...my God!
The MICROPHONE makes her voice jarring, gagged. She looks silently. No sobbing, no big sad looks. Just shock. Shock of recognition, shock of time gone by.
BILLY looking at her, his eyes moving down to:
BILLY P.O.V. - SUSAN, her neck, her breasts straining against the thin shirt.
SUSAN fingers the photo album nervously, speaking slow and distinct; not sure she is communicating.

SUSAN
...Billy, your family is fine.
Senator Buckley just made a special plea on your behalf in the Senate.
Newsday has written several big articles about you. They've called you a pawn in the poppy game between
Nixon and the Turks. The letters are coming in, Billy. People care....
Stops, shakes her head. It sounds all wrong in this context.
BILLY is still staring at her breasts. He hasn't seen a woman for five years and now a hungry animal look comes into his eyes He moves suddenly pressing up against the glass, rabid. And in Turkish:

BILLY
(in Turkish)
Take it off. Take it off!
(then remembering the English)
Take it off. Take it off!
His voice is savage, demanding.
SUSAN understands, startled. Looks around.

SUSAN
Billy - you'll just make yourself crazy.

BILLY
BILLY
Take it off! Take it off!
(suddenly in a very soft voice)
...S'il vous plait?...
A strange look in his eye.
SUSAN slowly, scared, begins to unbutton her shirt.
HAMIDOU looks on silently, does nothing.
BILLY follows every movement with wild-eyed lust.
SUSAN leans up close to the window. With both hands on the front of her blouse, she slowly draws it apart.
BILLY going wild! Against the window. His hand down in his pyjamas.
HER BREASTS spring free, quivering, full and ripe with a deep cleavage and hard dark nipples. They hang full and loose. FULL SCREEN

BILLY'S EYES - FULL SCREEN.
BILLY beats on the window, working his mouth soundlessly.
SUSAN is shattered, scared of Billy's sanity.

SUSAN
Oh Billy, Billy, I wish I could make it better for you. Please don't... don't...
Tears. Fear.
BILLY tightens dramatically and comes right in his pants, slumps against the window.
SUSAN realizes he has come, surprised.
BILLY looks at her. Furtive, animal shame. And suddenly he starts to cry. A flood of feelings locked up too long come pouring out. He murmurs some words, Turkish SOUNDS sputtering out in his throat, then:

BILLY
S.... Susan?
Softly, working his mouth finding it hard to speak.
SUSAN yearning. Tears sprinkling her eyes.

SUSAN
Yes, Billy?
BILLY straining, not out of physical weakness but an emotional one. Sputters, eyes closed.

BILLY
...I love you....
It sounds pathetic, lost.
SUSAN is worked up to the limit, tries to hug him through the window.

SUSAN
Oh Billy... Billy! Don't give up.
Please don't give up. You'll get out. I know you will!

Remembers something. Grabs the PHOTO ALBUM with all her strength, holding it up for him to see through the glass.Then remembering herself, looks around the room to make sure they're alone and in a contained voice:

SUSAN
Billy, your father gave me this for you. There's pictures of your
Mom and Dad...Rob...Peg...
BILLY looks at it listlessly.
HIS P.V.O - SUSAN holding the album open to PICTURES of his MOTHER and FATHER in front of the house, ROB on a bicycle, PEG in her cheer-leading outfit.

SUSAN
And there's pictures in the back of your old Mr. Franklin. Remember him... From the bank?
A certain tone slips into her voice.

SUSAN
He's over in Greece now. He bought a ticket.
BILLY looks from the album to Susan. Possibly there is a gleam of understanding in his eyes but it is very faint.
An Attendant BANGS on Susan's door, OFF.

VOICE
Visiting is over.
SUSAN quickly puts the album away as if it were a hidden weapon.

SUSAN
I'll give it to them for you.
She buttons her blouse but her eyes are worried, on Billy.

SUSAN
You were right Billy don't count on them, you hear, don't count on anybody but yourself!
The ATTENDANT now swings open her door, annoyed.

ATTENDANT
Let's go!
Susan stands, about to go, then suddenly leans up close to the bars, hard and practical.

SUSAN
(quickly)
If you stay you'll die Billy! Get out of here. Get to Greece, you hear me?...Billy?
Pause. Silence. She closes her eyes, in pain; she doesn't think she has reached him. She turns to go, resigned.
BILLY looking at her. Behind him HAMIDOU opens the door.
A calm and cunning look on his face, glancing with Billy towards

A BRIEF GLIMPSE of SUSAN looking back, the album under her arm. The door closes.

CUT:
BILLY, with the same deadened expression as before, comes down the STAIRS towards THE WHEEL. It is early morning and the walkers haven't started yet. Billy looks at the Pillar a dire look of reflection passing over his eyes. Then he starts walking but in a clockwise motion, opposite the normal pattern; in the same methodical manner as before.

ANOTHER ANGLE
BILLY, on the inner track, passes TWO LUNATICS who are walking counter-clockwise. They glare at him, motion for him to turn around. Billy just keeps walking. BILLY intersects several more LUNATICS going counter- clockwise They motion for him to turn.

LUNATIC
(grunting)
Gower!
Tries to block Billy's way, but BILLY shakes his head, brushes by him - determined. AHMET Slides up next to BILLY in his rags.

AHMET
Good morning, my American friend!
There will be trouble if you go this way. A good Turk always walks to the right. Left is communist.
Right is good. You must go the other way... It's Good.
More LUNATICS join the flow, gesturing or grunting at BILLY.
BILLY STOPS, turns, looks at the rest of them slogging in the usual direction, looks as if he 'sees' them; and he walks out of the wheel, towards the stairs.
AHMET curious about his unusual behavior, follows BILLY.

AHMET
Why you go? Why don't you walk the wheel with us?
(suspiciously leaning forward, suddenly realizing the answer)
The bad machine doesn't know he's a bad machine. You still don't believe it? You still don't believe you're a bad machine?

ANOTHER ANGLE
BILLY stops and turns to look at AHMET at the base of the STAIRS. BILLY carries on up the stairs.

AHMET
(shakes his head)
To know oneself is to know God, my friend. The factory knows. That's why they put you here. You'll see.

You'll find out. Later on you'll know.

BILLY stops and turns to look at AHMET. His eyes glint with special knowledge and he takes AHMET into his confidence using the latter's tone of voice:

BILLY

I already know. I know that you're a bad machine. That's why the factory keeps you here.

(Lowers s voice)

You know how I know? I know because

I'm from the factory. I make the machines.. I'm here to spy on you.

Eyes narrow. Surprise. Fear. He shuffles away.

BILLY looks at him and turns up the STAIRS.

CUT:

BILLY in his BED. The usual UPROAR. THE ATTENDANT comes by with the pills, offers a handful to BILLY.

ATTENDANT

Hop! Hop! Take!

He takes them, puts a few into his mouth, swallows.

Reflective, unsure. A RADIO playing OFF blares suddenly with the U.S. Armed Forces Station - JANIS JOPLIN singing

"Take another piece of my heat now, Baby" then it's switched back to a TURKISH STATION, loud. Billy rises.

BILLY enters the TOILET with the PHOTO ALBUM tightly clutched under his arm.

A dark stone room, very shadowy.

Piles of waste on the floor. A vacant-eyed barefoot LUNATIC shuffles past BILLY who goes to one of the four partitioned

HOLES cut into the floor.

ANOTHER ANGLE - BILLY squats over it and with his filthy long nails he starts to slit open the back binder of the album Susan gave him. Flickering shadows. He looks up absently.

THREE LUNATIC FACES stare in at him through wooden slats, tongues hanging out and drooling - playing with themselves -

OFF.

BILLY makes a lunatic face and SCREAM kicking at the partition.

BILLY

Aaaaaaaaaaaaaaaaaahhhhhhhhhhhhhhhh!!!

THE LUNATICS, petrified, scatter off but ONE LUNATIC skids in a puddle of urine and crashes onto the tile howling.

BILLY slits open the binder to reveal TEN HUNDRED DOLLAR

BILLS with Pictures of Mr. Franklin' neatly inserted.

ANOTHER ANGLE

BILLY has no particular expression on his face. Reflective, staring at the money; he looks up.

A LARGE SILHOUETTE is moving towards him.

BILLY just watches, transfixed, not trying to hide the money.

HAMIDOU comes into a faint light, looking down at him; glances at the money. Shakes his head gently.

HAMIDOU
No do! No do!
Reaches for and:
ANOTHER ANGLE - HAMIDOU takes the money from BILLY like candy from a baby, then takes him by the ear and slowly lifts him up. Billy is like a vegetable in his hands.

HAMIDOU
(in his broken
English)
I tell you I see 'gain...
(into Turkish)
I take you down to bath and your feet be big like...Breasts
(a gesture)
HAMIDOU leads BILLY roughly out of the lunatic room, pulling him by the ear.

HAMIDOU still Pulling BILLY by the ear, guides him through the GUARD QUARTERS.

HAMIDOU leads him up a narrow winding flight of STAIRS.

HAMIDO
First you make mistake with Ziat, now you make mistake with money.

You're not a new Prisoner, Vilyum

Hi-yes.

The tone of his voice indicates a severe reckoning this time.

HAMIDOU pulls BILLY by the ear into a large echoing BATH.

BILLY looking, bent over by the ear - a hint of awareness of new surroundings.

ANOTHER ANGLE - the BATH is deserted, spooky with greenish

Yellow fish light flittering down from holes in ceiling around damp mossy arches. Steam rises off a bath. Benches, buckets of water. HAMIDOU swings BILLY around until he is facing him.

HAMIDOU makes an elaborate gesture of putting aside his falaka stick and holstered gun; he will use his hands.

HAMIDOU
(shakes his head)
You've been in prison too long,
Vilyum Hi-yes.
He takes that: stiff arm all the way back to its full arc and WHACKS BILLY up against the wall.

BILLY bounces back off the wall. The print of Hamidou's fingers is imbedded like a flaring white rainbow in the redness of his left cheek. SLAM - a backhanded whack. BILLY bounces right back from the wall. steadies him.

HAMIDOU
You go crazy here Vilyum Hi-yes.
Many people go crazy here. Best thing for crazy people is this...
THE BLOW, in SLOW MOTION comes sailing into:
BILLY, and we see the brief boxer's distortion of all his face as he flies upwards and back into:
THE BENCH smashing it. Echo like jarring F.X.
BILLY is held up by the PAJAMAS, steadied. The Turkish words seem far away, incomprehensible.

HAMIDOU (OFF)
Vilyum Hi-yes. You die here, Hi- yes.
WHACK - ANOTHER BLOW, but:
HAMIDOU this time holds onto the pajamas using Billy like a punching bag.

WHACK - A REVERSE BLOW.
HAMIDOU increasingly excited.

HAMIDOU
Babba sikijam! I fuck your mother,
I fuck your sister...
WHACK - ANOTHER BLOW in SLOW MOTION

HAMIDOU
...I fuck your father, I fuck your brother...
RIP! - a loud SOUND as HAMIDOU moves with a blur of speed, and shreds BILLY's pajamas with his hands.
BILLY naked, totally passive, semiconscious. HAMIDOU suddenly shifts position and snaps Billy into a strenuous wrestling hold across his knee on the steamy floor. He loosens him up by cracking his bones along his back.
HAMIDOU - sweat pouring off his face, excited.

HAMIDOU
...And I fuck your grandmother and
I fuck your pretty girlfriend...
And I fuck you Hi-yes!)
A bizarre otherworldly scene. This man is dredging Billy through a sadistic imagination sparked by the steam, the sweat, and an ethnic identification with a Turkish steam bath as a bedroom. He loosens his hold abruptly, rises, moves off as:
BILLY holds himself on his knees, head sunk on his chest, gasping for breath, about to vomit. Pause; he looks up horrified at:
HAMIDOU pouring fresh buckets of water on the floor.

SSSSSSSSSS! The awakened STEAM coils like a snake into every cranny of the little room.
BLURRED VISUALS - HAMIDOU stripping his shirt off. A huge muscular flash of chest,
A BELT being snapped open.
BILLY waiting.
A FIGURE moving through the steam, closer.
BILLY backing away from it.
STEAM - a glint of a FACE coming through. HAMIDOU - his eyes so intense they seem to burn off the steam like sun cutting haze. Then disappear again.
BILLY pulls back. A pause. Silence. Cat and mouse. Then very suddenly:
A HAND reaches out of the STEAM and GRABS BILLY by the hair. A GRUNT, OFF. BILLY his eyes moving fast.
A FLASH of a huge darkened penis, fully erect cutting forward into the steam like a from drill, detached from the rest of the body.
A SOUND - grotesque and so sudden after the silence it jars the senses. A BLURRED VISUAL then:
BILLY Launching forward in SLOW MOTION, desperation distorting his features and:
STEAM - then BILLY'S HEAD SLAMS through it in SLOW MOTION and:
SMASHES the penis with its skull. A horrifying GASP.
BLURRED VISUALS - STEAM - HAMIDOU staggering CLOSE - surprise, pain...

BILLY MOVING.
A FOOT coming up fast through the steam, connecting again with the genitals. Another SCREAM.
A BODY hitting the tiles.
BILLY groping for the falaka stick. Raises it.
A STRUGGLE - Two bodies thrashing, one of them screaming now in pain. A definitive sound then a THWACK! Another thwack! The steam seems to clear and BILLY is on top of the gigantic HAMIDOU smashing him with the falaka stick with all his might.
HAMIDOU is in contortions, his nose busted and bleeding.
His HAND gripping BILLY by the neck, forcing him back and strangling him at the same time. Billy is red in the face, such is the force of this creature but continues to beat him, harder, harder. His expression filled with a life energy, seeded in hatred, that he thought he had lost.
Again, Again -

BILLY
Babba sikijam, Hamidu! I fuck your
Mother, I fuck your daughter, I fuck your sons, I fuck your wife!
The BAND slips from his throat, then springs up desperately again and clenches Billy's whole face with one gigantic palm, clawing to get in, then just as quickly slips away.
BILLY beats on - again, again.
BLOOD flows fast in agitated swirls into the little pool.

CUT:

BILLY opens a door gently, moves across an empty CORRIDOR, dressed in and gun in intense. Hamidou's holster. large uniform with his He looks shaken, weak, falaka stick dizzy but

VOICE (OFF)
How about a shoe shine, friend?
BILLY starts, clenches the falaka stick ready to spring, spins.
A LITTLE SHOESHINE BOY is his case down the corridor.
BILLY has not seen a child in a long time. get words out, then manages: Surprised.
Can't get the words out, then manages:

BILLY
No!
THE KID shrugs, moves on, looking At Billy strangely.
BILLY goes up a flight of STAIRS. Ahead, VOICES passing.
He stops. Goes on.
BILLY goes through an empty GUARD QUARTERS.
BILLY is in another CORRIDOR, approaches
A SMALL PORTAL, daylight at its edges. Locked?
BILLY, tense, tries it. It swings open on:

DAYLIGHT!
BILLY squints. Adjusting to the harsh sensation.

AN ISTANBUL STREET - TRAFFIC, SOUNDS. TWO GUARDS approaching the portal in the distance, drinking soda pop.
BILLY steps back, straightens his clothes, steps out briskly and at such an angle that THE TWO GUARDS don't notice him in the traffic as they enter the open portal.
LONG SHOT - BILLY walking down the street, looking back, almost bewildered, not quiet believing this.

CUT:
TIGHT - RAILROAD TICKET being stamped. SOUND - SNAP.
MOVE UP to TICKET CLERK behind a grill.

VOICE (OFF)
Edirne to Uzun Kopru?
THE CLERK looks puzzled.
BILLY is on the other side of the grill. A ill-fitting new Western style suit, a hat over his dyed black hair; totally paranoid. He hasn't slept in three days and the bruises from the Hamidou beating now show clearly black and blue on his face. His eyes are alert, darting around, his speech clipped and to the point.

BILLY
What's the matter?

THE CLEF!! Shrugs.

CLERK
'What are you crazy? There's no train anymore to Uzun Kopru, it'd have to go through Greece. The border's closed.
BILLY taken by surprise.

BILLY
No train?

CLERK (OFF)
No more train.
BILLY Moves off a small provincial RAILROAD DEPOT - DAY.
He looks at the:
EMPTY TRACKS - No 'midnight express'.

CUT:
BILLY, tenser than ever, uses the occasion of buying a newspaper at an OUTDOOR STAND to study:
THE MAIN SQUARE of the VILLAGE (EDIRNE) - DAY. SOLDIERS and POLICE are abundant, chattering bustling amid tanks and half-tracks. Mountains can be seen in the far distance.
BILLY camouflages his face as best he can in the Newspaper
"Hurriyet" studying:
CABDRIVERS in the Main Square. Most of them are older, grizzled looking standing next to their old battered dusty cabs talking with stray SOLDIERS. Billy's eyes settle on a
YOUNGER DRIVER with longish hair, possibly an ally.
BILLY glances down at his newspaper as a SOLDIER intersects and his expression goes stony as he sees:
FULL COLOR DRAWING (first page) of a ridiculously fierce heavy-muscled barechested MAN beating a facsimile of Hamidou into the ground. Next to it a blurry badly reproduced photograph of BILLY with a superimposed GUN in his hand.
You can't really tell it's him.
BILLY, controlling himself, crumples up the newspaper into a baton, his eyes everywhere. Be the darting A crosses square.
ANOTHER ANGLE - BILLY, intersecting a POLICEMAN who glances at him, joins the YOUNG CABDRIVER..

BILLY
Listen, I have Swedish friends camping south of the town. I was supposed to meet them here this morning but I was late. Can you take me there?
DRIVER looks at him neutral.

DRIVER
You know where they are?

BILLY
(anxious to get in the cab)
Sure.

DRIVER
How far?

BILLY
(impatient)
About ten kilometers.

DRIVER
Sixty Lira?

BILLY
(surprised)
Sixty?
Billy eyes:

APPROACHING SOLDIERS.
BILLY (OFF)
Okay.
THE DRIVER, noticing Billy's look at the soldiers, gets in the cab.
BILLY climbs into the back seat, feeling already he has made a mistake. There is something too alert, too hard in this young driver.

CUT:
BILLY P.O.V. - THE MOUNTAINS as they roll in the taxi.

FORESTS - FIELDS.
INTERIOR TAXI
BILLY
Those mountains? are they?

DRIVER
(Greece
(shakes his head)
Very bad now. Maybe war. Those
Greek pigs try to steal Cyprus again
(pause))
How'd you lose your friends?
BILLY leaning back in his seat, casual.

BILLY
Oh, I drank a lot of raka last night in Istanbul. Got into a fight.

Indicates the bruises on his face.
DRIVER looking at him in the rear view mirror. His curiosity narrowing.

DRIVER
How come you speak Turkish so good?
BILLY casually glances out the window.

BILLY
Did twenty months in prison in
Istanbul. Hash
THE DRIVER studies BILLY in the rear-view mirror. Then:

DRIVER
You want to score some? Cheap?
BILLY looks at him hard. Something's wrong with this man.

BILLY
(curt)
No!
Cutting off further conversation, he looks out at:
THE MOUNTAINS of Greece - with longing.
BILLY stares back at:
THE DRIVER whose eyes now move away from the rear-view mirror under the pressure of the stare. SOUND OFF loud machinery.
BILLY turning - in rear window, we see a TURKISH HALFTRACK pulling alongside the cab, SOLDIERS waving their arms for the cabdriver to get out of the way.
ANOTHER ANGLE - the HALFTRACK pulls level. The CABDRIVER slows down, with a curse.
BILLY - beads of sweat trickle his brow
THE PERSONNEL CARRIER, disinterested, pulls past.
BILLY breathes heavily with nervous relief.

CUT:
THE CAB pulls up to the end of a dirt road.
BILLY has his MAP out, studying it.

BILLY
The Maritas River? Where is it?
ANOTHER ANGLE - the DRIVER, exasperated, waves southwest.

DRIVER
Two miles! Minefields over there.
Do you know where this campground is or not?

BILLY
Not far. Just a little way.

DRIVER
No! I'm not going any further!
It'll wreck my car.

BILLY
I'll pay extra

DRIVER
How much?
ANOTHER ANGLE - BILLY slips him fifty lira. The DRIVER takes it, muttering
under his breath, jams the cab into gear.
THE CAB follows rutted tracks into low HILLS.
INTERIOR CAB - very bumpy.

BILLY
Where are the minefields?

DRIVER
All over. Turkish Army up there.
It's against the law. They shoot us.
(looks up in the mirror)
You sure you looking for your friends, man?

BILLY(VERY SHARP NOW)
(very sharp now)
Okay! Ley me out right here. I'm getting tired of all this bullshit from you. I'll walk it.

DRIVER
(looks back, then ahead, suddenly brightening)
Ah, look! they probably know where the campers are
BILLY's entire expression changes. It is all over.
A TANK AND HALFTRACK are sitting there by the rutted track, with SOLDIERS.
And a little LEAN-TO with several POLICE.
Also a couple of attack DOGS on leashes. The Driver honks his horn on the approach.

ANOTHER ANGLE
DRIVER
Hey officer, we're looking for the campground. Do you know where it is?
ANOTHER ANGLE - TWO POLICEMEN and A SOLDIER come sauntering over,
their collars open, beer bottles in hand, slightly drunk.

POLICEMAN
(curt)
You're not supposed to be here

DRIVER
(indicated Billy)
He's a tourist, what do you want, he says he's looking for friends at the campground.
FIRST POLICEMAN glances BILLY

POLICEMAN
Campground?
(shrugs)
Never heard of one.

DRIVER
Seen any Swedish foreigners in a camper-bus?
SECOND POLICEMAN meanwhile eases his arm down on the OPEN
WINDOW bringing BILLY into foreground. The COP'S mouth is open and exhaling a
wave of beer breath over-BILLY.
BILLY P.O.V. - BEER FACE FOCUS PAST him to SOLDIER at tank reading
"Hurriyet" - the picture of BILLY on page one, spread for all to see.

BEER FACE
Noldu?
DRIVER turning around to address him.

DRIVER
Seen any foreigners in a camper bus?
SOLDIER circles the cab from the other side.
BILLY motions to the DRIVER.

BILLY
Okay, they haven't seen him, let's go back to town, it's getting late.
THE DRIVER ignores it. Calls out again, louder to BEER

FACE.
DRIVER
Foreigners! KAMPER. VOLKSWAGEN
BILLY rigid. This asshole of a driver!
BEER FACE glances at BILLY, pulls his head out the window.
Looks down the road. Takes a sip of beer.
SOLDIER, disinterested, moves back towards the tank.
BEER FACE looks in the other direction down the road, burps. Very conscious of his
authority, shakes his head without looking at the driver. Moves away.
BILLY nudges the DRIVER.

BILLY
Okay, let's go.
THE DRIVER impatiently turns and looks straight at BILLY, aware of his anxiety.

DRIVER

Is no Volkswagen, man! Something wrong with you?
BILLY hardening.
DRIVER calling out.
BEER FACE turns.
DRIVER leans out the window.

DRIVER

This guy's fishy...I think he might be trying to get to Greece.
BILLY looks around fast.
BEER FACE starts back lazily, half drunk, with the OTHER

POLICEMAN
BEER FACE

Huh?

DRIVER
DRIVER

I don't know, there's
His eyes grow big suddenly As he sees the barrel of
Hamidou's REVOLVER right in His cheek.
BILLY all business, very quiet.

BILLY

Get out -- right now, move!
BEER-FACE advancing looks puzzled, thinks he sees something, then crouches as:
DRIVER gets out the door crouching, yells.

DRIVER

He's got a gun!
BILLY firing SHOTS off to distract them has climbed over the front seat, jams the cab into gear. It stalls! Again he tries, and now shoots off.
THE CAB Roars past the roadblock.
THE COPS AND SOLDIER, scattered by the shots, now scream at each other. They run. SHOTS are fired.
BILLY guns the cab down the road, flying.
CLOUDS OF DUST trail the cab.
THE TANK starts to roll after it. Full speed. The HALFTRACK follows, the MEN riding it shouting.
BILLY looks back, then looking ahead sees something.
P.O.V - a speck in the far distance. Another ROADBLOCK.
BILLY decides, then -
THE CAB swerves right off the road and jumps into the gently rolling FIELD on the border of the road, pock marked with

HILLS.

THE TURKS come roaring down the road, pointing to the cab.
LOW ANGLE - the TANK makes a flat out stop, gears grinding.
THE GUN TURRET swings left.
THE CAB in the far distance, at an angle to the tank, starts running up an incline.

THE TANK FIRES.
P.O.V. - SHELL BLASTS WIDE OF THE CAB.
BILLY, startled, looks back, guns for the top of the incline.
HIS P.O.V. - ANOTHER SHELL now blasts to his front right, closer. Something heavy (shrapnel) thuds into the rood of the cab.
BILLY drives all out.

P.O.V. - THE INCLINE CLOSER, CLOSER, ABOUT TO MAKE IT, THEN: A BLAST
TANK P.O.V. - the CAB spinning in the blast of the adjacent shell-burst.
BILLY, shaken but unhurt, staggers out of the cab, looks:

P.O.V. - A WHEEL BLASTED AWAY, FUEL PISSING OUT FROM THE SHRAPNEL HOLES, SMASHED WINDSHIELD AND FENDER.
THE TURKS are coming up the incline now, like the Cavalry -- some on foot running, others on the HALFTRACK. BULLETS whistle and pop nearby.
BILLY running. He tears off his jacket.
SOLDIERS pass the wrecked car, at the top of the incline shouting, pointing and firing at
BILLY in the distance.
ONE SOLDIER seems lighter than the others and takes off in a sprint as the OTHERS follow.
THE HALFTRACK now crests the incline and gathering full gear and momentum, roars off down the slope after Billy.
CLOSE BILLY running sweat all over him. In background, the
HALFTRACK and running FIGURES.
BILLY runs into a high dry cornfield with the sun starting to set ahead of him in the Greek mountains.
MOUNTAINS - must make those mountains.
BILLY running all out - eyes fixed on them, breathing, skipping heartbeats.
THE PERSONNEL CARRIER bypasses the FAST SOLDIER who slows down, panting. Billy has outrun him.
OTHER SOLDIERS run up in the distance.
BILLY, tireless, obsessed, runs right into a POPPY FIELD.It is a splendid beautiful scarlet red, set off by the dipping rays of the sun.
HIS FEET smashing down the poppy plants. Fast - THUCK!

THUCK! THUCK! THUCK! THUCK! THUCK!
CROSSCUT the metal TREADS of the Halftrack into the poppy, mowing down entire rows.

TWO SOLDIERS on the PERSONNEL CARRIER are waving encouragement to the driver inside. They have him.
ANOTHER ANGLE the HALFTRACK closing the distance on BILLY now thirty yards apart.
BILLY looking back, starting to fade. Huge wheezing gasps of breath.
SOLDIERS running up looking at
THE HALFTRACK in the distance.
SOLDIERS yell.

SOLDIERS
Minefield! Minefield! Come back!
Stop!

(NO SUBTITLE)
BILLY runs out of the POPPY FIELD into a THIN FOREST.
THE SOLDIERS screaming in the distance, jumping up and down waving for the halftrack to come back.
LOW ANGLE - the HALFTRACK with the waving SOLDIERS on board now blasts out of the poppy field at full speed.
BILLY -- he has no chance, In immediate background is the fast HALFTRACK.
ONE SOLDIER on the HALFTRACK now looking back to the SHOUTS of his comrades. Confused. Turns bout back to yell something and:
ENORMOUS EXPLOSION The HALFTRACK disintegrates in a tank landmine.
BILLY thrown to the ground by the force of the blast, looks back, GASPS!
A BURNING WRECKAGE. Black spirals of smoke. Secondary explosions.
BILLY stumbles up. A gash of blood is on his temple but he doesn't know it or feel it such is his stress. He runs on,
SHOTS whistling towards him from the poppy field.
TURKISH OFFICER screaming angrily at Billy, cursing, shaking his fist at the sky.
BILLY, in the forest, is totally out of breath and out of eyesight of the pursuers. He stops against a tree. FROG
SOUNDS. The gurgle of water. Muddy ground. He looks:
THE MARITAS RIVER rushing ahead. A strong current.
BILLY peels off all his clothing except his pants, not delaying one more moment. He feels he must keep going. And he's right. DOGS are barking OFF.
A SNARLING ATTACK DOG is tearing through the minefield, fast, ahead of the others.
BILLY looks, sees it.
THIRTY YARDS - the huge DOG coming right at him!
BILLY runs for the edge of the bank and plunges in.
THE ATTACK DOG sprints up to the edge of the river bank and without a moment's hesitation, plunges right in after him.
BILLY lashing into the current with a fierce breast stroke, is swept downstream kicking futilely.
THE DOG, its jaws open and clacking, is also swept down river.
BILLY going under, coming back up - fighting, still fighting.

THE DOG struggling sails past as

BILLY hauls himself out of the river, going in a circle, dizzy. Falls. Struggles up again. Looks back. Must keep going. Must.

THE BASE OF' MOUNTAIN - hilly, rugged.

BILLY runs, drags, runs again. He is a lamentable sight - naked except for ripped wet pants, barefoot, bleeding, muddied. Dimly he makes out:

A FARMHOUSE - TWILIGHT. Some cows, goats, chickens. NO sign of people.

BILLY staggers towards it. Wears something. A rooting SOUND.

Stops. Something familiar about it.

A FAMILY OF PIGS snort and root in the mud, little piglets running around.

BILLY staggers towards them, muttering to himself.

BILLY
Pigs...! Pigs...!
Then yells in the recognition of it

BILLY
Pigs... You... Beautiful...
BILLY BILLY falls to his knees in the confined pen; the pigs run around squealing. Trying to reach out for one of them, he falls face first into the mud and lies there.
Pause. A wooden DOOR squeaks open OFF. BILLY slowly turns his muddy eyes over his shoulder.
BILLY P.O.V. - TWO SOLDIERS, khaki-colored uniforms, helmets, olive faces, mustaches, approach cautiously from the farmhouse, rifles ready. Following them is an OLD
FARMER, Further behind in the doorway is his WIFE and

CHILDREN.
BILLY muttering to himself, in Turkish.

BILLY
Greek?... Greek?...
THE SOLDIERS approach close, stand above this strange figure, look at each other.

SOLDIER
Ti leei?
(What is he saying?)

2ND SOLDIER
Mou fainetai san Toupkika
(It sounded like Turkish)
BILLY with dimming strength.

BILLY
THE FARMER understands, makes a vigorous nod of his head.

FARMER
Malisee...Ellada!
(Ah, yes... Greece!)

CUT:
CAR DOOR SLAMS SHUT - and BILLY, his movements still weak, moves a few steps from the car and stops. SUBTITLE:

OCTOBER 24, 1975 - BABYLON, LONG ISLAND
Framing Billy are SUSAN and his FATHER, both silent. They look with him at
HIS SISTER, BROTHER, UNCLE, AUNT, SISTER-In-LAW FAMILY
FRIEND - AND GRANDMOTHER, all on the porch of the ordinary house in BABYLON, LONG ISLAND - DAY; all of them returning his gaze in that first SILENT moment. Curiosity.
Recognition. Shock. Love.
And then they move. But we don't hear their movements. It is SOUNDLESS reunion; the SISTER running out first in SLOW
MOTION, the MOTHER following last, crying; the GRANDMOTHER too infirm to move, the shaking her head from side to side in SLOW MOTION, her tears lost somewhere in the wrinkles of her face.
BILLY surrounded by FAMILY - SLOW MOTION - SOUNDLESS. His eyes flooding. All the feelings in him. And deep inside - a solitary question.

EPILOGUE BLACK SCREEN - SUPERIMPOSE:
THE CHARACTER NAMED BELL IS STILL INSIDE.
AS ARE:
(ROLL THE LIST OF NAMES)
And OVER this, the SOUND of a PASSING TRAIN rushing by in the night - UP, FAST and AWAY.
(Getchmis Olsun)

THE END

Printed in Great Britain
by Amazon

25082065R00057